Landscapes
of Ireland

CLB 1260
© 1986 Illustrations and text: Colour Library Books Ltd.,
   Guildford, Surrey, England.
Text filmsetting by Acesetters Ltd., Richmond, Surrey, England.
All rights reserved.
Published 1986 by Crescent Books, distributed by Crown Publishers, Inc.
Printed in Spain.
ISBN 0 517 46289 3
h g f e d c b a

Landscapes of Ireland

Text by

Terence Sheehy

Featuring the photography of
CLIVE FRIEND

CRESCENT BOOKS
NEW YORK

Ireland, off-shore island of an off-shore island, perched precariously on the very edge of the continental shelf at the far western end of the land mass that is Europe, lies, a staggeringly beautiful Green Isle, between 51½ degrees to 55½ degrees latitude north, and 5½ degrees and 10½ degrees longitude west. This tiny and magical treasure island is only 32,595 square miles, with its greatest length from north to south of 302 miles, and its greatest width from east to west of 171 miles. There are coasts ranging from the tumultuous, warm waters of the Gulf Stream sweeping down the entire length of the Atlantic west coast, to the soft swelling waters of the Irish Sea on the eastern seaboard. No place in Ireland is more than 80 miles from the sea, and its rugged fjord or sandy-beached coastline extends for about 2,000 lovely miles.

The pure, clear white light of the rain-rinsed, 'Impressionist' skies, and the physical features of the many and varied landscapes, have fashioned and moulded a unique race of island people, deeply moved by the elements, who have become intoxicated with the words of everyday conversation and have spelt them out in a riot of imaginative literature and bewildering poetry. The landscapes that make the Irish people so articulate are of a thousand lakes and mountains and rivers and salmon pools. The highest mountain, Carrantuohill, at 3,314 feet, deep south in the province of Munster, in the Kingdom of Kerry, looks fixedly west to the next parish, America, 2,400 miles away. From Fair Head, in the Province of Ulster, in the north of the country, the view from the basalt and chalk cliffs is across the windswept heather and the rolling seas to the Mull of Kintyre, a stone's throw away in Scotland.

To the south, the gentle round of the coast forms the eastern side of the St George's Channel, some 50 miles from Wales, and the blue Wicklow Mountains rising above the parkland county of Ireland stare steadfastly across the Irish sea, 50 or 60 miles to their sister mountains, the Caledonian range of Wales.

The Irish mountains and hills are mainly coastal, standing guard over a large, central, saucer-shaped lowland plain of limestone. Down from the north pours the River Shannon, the largest river in these off-shore islands of Europe, over 230 miles in length, draining one fifth of the entire landscape of Ireland, before disgorging itself into the Atlantic Ocean, like a minor Yangtze-Kiang, between the county of Clare on the north bank and the county of Kerry on the south bank. Vast and many are the lakes of Ireland, the largest being Lough Neagh, 153 square miles, 17 miles long and 11 miles broad, fed by the waters of the Upper and the Lower Bann, in the county of Antrim.

Because of its far, far westerly position on the edge of the Continental Shelf, the sundials of the west of Ireland are at least 30 minutes slower than those of Greenwich, and there always seems to be that extra hour of pure, white light each evening on the Atlantic coast of Ireland. The dawn comes up earlier too, and the climate during the day is always moderate because of the influence of the surrounding seas. The flora is rich, ranging from Arctic-alpine to Mediterranean species of wild flowers. Because of the warming effect of the Gulf Stream the vegetation of the Atlantic coastal regions, particularly of County Cork and County Kerry, is in many cases semi-tropical. The fauna includes 380 species of wild birds, Irish deer, unusual stoats and mountain hares, and unique frogs, toads and newts and lizards, but no snakes. There is an abundance of fish: game fish such as salmon and trout, lakes and rivers teeming with coarse fish such as pike, rudd, bream, roach and dace, and sea fish which include pollack, plaice, ray, bass and whiting, with deep sea fish such as basking shark, giant skate and monk-fish. Off the west coast the dolphins play in the warm waters of the Gulf Stream, and on the islands of Ireland seals abound in peace and plenty.

Man is the product of his environment, and the Irishman, isolated from the rest of Europe, and far from the New World, has been greatly influenced by the landscapes that surround him, to become a figure of enormous sensitivity, revelling in the beauty of nature, attuned to the world of the sun, moon and stars, and profoundly moved by the magic and mystery of all that is creation, 'rolled round the earth's diurnal course with rocks and stones and trees.'

Because of its sensuous, soft beauty, incredible charm and strange pagan magic, Ireland has always been regarded by the Irish as 'Mother' Ireland, the 'She' figure, the female goddess, the hidden love spoken of as a Queen, as 'Kathleen, the daughter of Houlihane', as the 'Dark Rosaleen,' and by a host of other poetic and secret names.

Arguably one of the most effective propaganda posters of the modern era of Irish politics was a picture of the map of Ireland, within whose outline knelt the figure of a young girl, with her back to England, and with her arms stretched out in supplication to the New World, pleading for her freedom.

For those less enthusiastic about the young girl with 'The walk of a Queen,' it is a sobering thought that when the Atlantic breakers roll and crash their way onto the long, rocky western seaboard of the Emerald Isle, and fling themselves into spray over 400 feet high, they are reaching just about as high as this jewel of an island stands in general above sea level. Raise the surrounding seas by a mere 400 to 500 feet and Ireland of the Welcomes will largely disappear from the map of Europe, and the face of the earth.

Trace the anatomy of the landscapes of Ireland and it will readily be seen that she is geologically more a sister to Scotland and to Wales than to England. She has affinities with some of the highlands of England, she must have been at some time in history wedded to the neighbouring off-shore island, and before that to Brittany. The geology of Ireland is such that her glacially formed landscape obligingly sheered off all her rich coal deposits but left others as a gift for all time to her flirtatious and domineering neighbour, England. The consequences are that Ireland today retains her truly rural and bucolic charm of landscape, and England has been transformed by an Industrial Revolution that brought about her large cities and towns of today, and industrialised her

landscape to make economic and cultural contrasts and differences which make the Sceptred Isle a go-ahead twentieth century nation of atomic power stations and U.S. missile bases. Meanwhile, the Green Isle remains, largely, England in aspic, with a leisurely pace of life, which works on the theory that when God made time, he made plenty of it, and that one day the luck of the Irish will turn as they strike it rich with a Celtic sea oil bonanza to replace their endless and appropriate strikes of natural gas.

The landscapes of Ireland today sustain a population, in the Four Ancient Provinces of Ulster, Munster, Leinster and Connacht and in the 32 counties, of some 5 million people. In neighbouring England there are over one million Irish-born, and in the New World some 20 million of Irish ancestry.

From Giraldus Cambrensis writing in the 12th century until George Bernard Shaw writing in our time, the skies, the air, the very atmosphere of Ireland have an inexplicable and remarkable influence over people, so well put by G.B.S. when he wrote:

'There is no magic like that of Ireland,
there are no skies like Irish skies,
there is no air like Irish air,
the Irish climate will make the stiffest
and slowest mind flexible for life.'

Giraldus Cambrensis, on his visit to Ireland in A.D. 1187 as secretary to Prince John, son of King Henry II, wrote of 'The Many Good Points of the Island, and the Natural Qualities of the Country,'

'This is the most temperate of all countries. Cancer does not here drive you to take shade from its burning heat; nor does the cold of Capricorn send you rushing to the fire. You will seldom see snow here, and then it lasts only for a short time. But cold weather does not come with all the winds here, not only from the west, north-west and north, but also equally from the east, the Favonius and the Zephyr. Nevertheless, they are all moderate winds and none of them is too strong. The grass is green in the fields in winter, just the same as in summer. Consequently the meadows are not cut for fodder, nor do they ever build stalls for their beasts. The country enjoys the freshness and mildness of spring almost all the year round.

'The air is so healthy that there is no disease-bearing cloud, or pestilential vapour, or corrupting breeze. The island has little use for doctors... the air that we encompass by breathing in and which continually encompasses us, is guaranteed to be kindly and health-giving.'

And it was the Elizabethan poet, Edmund Spenser, who wrote of Ireland, 'a most beautiful and sweet country as any under Heaven; seamed through with many goodly rivers replenished with all sorts of fish, most abundantly sprinkled with many sweet islands and goodly lakes...'

So in climate and natural beauty, things have not changed that much over hundreds of years.

The anatomy of the landscapes of Ireland had an all-important bearing and influence on the type of people who came to inhabit this verdant island. Before we can talk of the Celts, the Vikings, the Anglo-Irish Normans, the Elizabethans, the Orangemen, the Young Irelanders, and in fact before we can use the term 'Irishman' or 'Irishwoman' at all, we have to look at the basic forms of the landscapes, that is, the underlying geology that goes to make up the thousand lakes, mountains and rivers, and the lowlands, the plains, the boglands and the coastlands and grasslands. Care has to be taken not to be influenced by the benefit of hindsight in making this approach to see how the present unique landscape of Ireland finally came about its fashioning of peoples.

Basically, the oldest rocks are at the bottom of the pile; the results of enormous pressures and foldings and contortions over millions of years. These various and ancient geological rock formations are then further separated into sedimentary rocks laid down as sea deposits of limestone, of gravels, of sands and various mixtures of mud in which there has been animal and plant life. From the study of the fossils in the various strata comes a scale in time which suggests periods of rock-time in millions of years of formation which bring back to mind our school geography class days in which we learnt of carboniferous rocks, those of coal and limestone and shale and sandstone, igneous rocks, of granite and volcanic origin, and the various rocks known as New Red Sandstone, Old Red Sandstone, Tertiary, Chalk, Silurian, Cambrian, and so on.

Like the High Kings of Ireland who swung around the country with their cohorts once a year on a march to extract tributes and to show who was boss, it is worthwhile pursuing a brief geological swing around the island with occasional sideways sorties to see just how the landscape helped to mould the people. Starting in the nearest land point to Scotland, the Antrim Plateau is the most north-easterly corner of Ireland. North of the present-day city of Belfast, it is immediately recognisable as igneous rock, as basalt country, over 1,500 square miles of it with steep cliff coastlines, the most famous of which are known today as the Giant's Causeway. This is but a few miles from Bush Mills, where Ireland's most splendid 12-year-old whiskey has been distilled from the earliest days. But more of this anon. Suffice to say that the Giant of the Causeway, Finn MacCool, is reported to have drunk of this 'water of life' as he built the causeway, about 13 miles across, which was to have joined the Scots with the Irish. While still wondering how on earth the Giant's Causeway produced its exact hexagonal columns of rock, the landscape and coastal strip of Antrim is a mass of the most beautiful glens and mountains, the latter including Trostan (1,817 feet high), Slievenanee (1,782), Slieveanorra (1,676), Slemish (1,436) and Agnew's Hill (1,675). The rivers in the glens tend to plunge into waterfalls, and valley floors have become a patchwork quilt of tilled fields.

The largest lake in Ireland, Lough Neagh, 153 square miles,

covers a sunken lava plain of Antrim, fed by the upper and lower Bann Rivers, and is part of that most exquisite landscape of the garden of Ulster. The apple-orchard lands of the county of Armagh touch on Lough Neagh which also shares its boundaries with the counties of Derry and Down. Turning West to Lough Foyle and to the counties of Derry and of Donegal, the quartzite metamorphic rock of these counties is shot through with granite and makes for a gleaming white, rugged landscape of mountains like miniature Fujiyamas. The natural geographical trend of all things in Donegal in its most northerly half is west to east towards Lough Foyle, and to what has now become the city of Derry, making the counties of Donegal and of Tyrone a continuous whole, a oneness with its geological and geographical natural links. The two enormous glacial loughs of Lough Foyle and Lough Swilly, which together help to make the Fjord Inishowen peninsula, are the start of what is probably the most beautiful, scenically, of the 32 counties of Ireland: the blue, lazy, rolling, mountainous county of Donegal. The most north-easterly coast of Donegal faces the untroubled, pure waters of the Atlantic Ocean spreading north as a silver sheen until it meets the cool waters of the Arctic Ocean of the North Pole itself. This spectacular fjord coast of pre-Cambrian quartzite rock includes Malin Head, Dunaff Head, Fanad, Mulroy Bay, Rosguill, Sheephaven, Horn Head, Bloody Foreland, Aranmore Island, Tory Island, Gweebarra Bay and Slieve League, all virtually unknown, even today, other than to the local inhabitants. A vast, blue county of lakes and streams and rivers, smashed by enormous rocks and boulders strewn over the landscape, Donegal is a mass of hidden glens and winding valleys with turf-covered lowlands, the whole transformed not only by the ice age of millions of years ago but dramatically fretted by the rolling Atlantic waves. Mount Errigal, the quartzite cone mountain of north Donegal, is really the Irish Fujiyama in appearance, and yet is quite easily approached and climbed.

The nature of Donegal is tiny, scattered hamlets hardened by Atlantic breezes and Arctic waters and yet ablaze with sunshine, particularly in the months of May and June because of its most northern and westerly position on the map of Europe.

Donegal is basically a north-south thrust of a county, with the spectacular and lovely Barnesmore Gap at the connecting axis between north and south. Memorable as the Blue Stack Granite mountains of Barnsmore are, arguably the most spectacular scenery in Ireland is the quartzite sea-cliff peninsula of Slieve League, reckoned by many to be the most beautiful and precipitous of sea cliffs in Europe, rising in one place to a knife-edge Eagle's Nest very nearly 2,000 feet high.

South of Donegal is the massive complex of water and turf-bog which dominates the county of Fermanagh in the shape of Lough Erne, which has an influence over 1,500 square miles of surrounding countryside. This is limestone and shale country and of no great beauty, and the same may be said of the land formation which gave rise to the city of Belfast, in the county of Antrim on the River Lagan. Dour is the word for this region.

South of here the isolated and fertile area of County Down, with its small, natural harbours which became associated with St Patrick, begins to get interesting. Famous in song, the Mountains of Mourne, where they 'sweep down to the sea', are indeed spectacular, as are the wide waters of Carlingford Lough. Again, this is isolated country of High Mournes and Low Mournes and the Kingdom of Mourne bordering the sea and Carlingford Lough. This is rich land, over 56 square miles of it. These mountains in County Down rise to 2,000 feet, with Slieve Donard at about 3,000 feet above the sea at Newcastle scenically magnificent.

Oversimplified in the school geography books as 'saucer-shaped', the Central Lowland areas of Ireland, with the town of Athlone on the Shannon in the middle, cover over 8,000 square miles of not the most scenically attractive landscape in the world. From a geological satellite it would appear as one whacking mass of largely uninteresting Carboniferous limestone, shale and sandstone, constituting very largely the massive boglands of Ireland. However, all is not lost, as the Province of Leinster is enormously rich in soils which make for the most prosperous lands in Ireland, namely the fat cattle pastures of County Meath and the rich green limestone plateau of Kildare, which breeds the finest racehorses in the world.

Dublin, on the River Liffey, on the eastern seaboard, has become the capital of Ireland and has been a major settlement on the hill above the River Liffey from pre-historic times until the present day. Because of its peculiar history in the hands of various occupying powers, Dublin was historically the nerve centre from which offensive or defensive forces radiated like the fingers of a hand. There were many times when these radiating fingers of offense or defence did not reach out very far, and finally they were withdrawn from Dublin altogether.

North of Dublin, little known or recognised except by archaeological historians, is the valley of the Boyne, with the most fabulous underground dwellings and tumuli and pre-Christian lunar observatories in Europe, such as those at Newgrange, in County Meath and at Dowth and at Knowth.

Also in County Meath is the hill of Tara, the third century base of the High Kings of Ireland. At Slane, a hill just 500 feet high is the site associated with the lighting in Ireland of the first Paschal Fire by St Patrick, at a point from which it could be seen by half-a-dozen Irish counties.

The boglands of central Ireland probably date from around 6,000 years B.C. and their coverage of the surface of Ireland today provides fuel for 'turf'-fired power-stations which supply over 10,000 million units of electricity for the 26 counties, about one quarter of the total electrical energy needed, and these kilowatt hours of energy employ almost 12,500 people in their production.

Immediately east of the central plain of boglands are the mile upon mile of watery lands which constitute the land mass and Lough Carrib area north of Galway city. This Connemara country is quite distinct from the landscapes of Donegal, of Antrim and the rest of the historical province of Ulster, and in sharp contrast to the features of Dublin and the province of Leinster. Galway spells lines of soft, blue mountains, with bundled up clouds floating in like galleons from the Western Atlantic, dark pools, banks of black and brown turf and bare mountainsides. Trees are few, some spruce and elm and yew and hazel, and an abundance of soggy bogland and rushes and dark brown gurgling and splashing mountain torrents and streams. The hallmark of Connemara is its twelve Bens or 'Pins', twelve cone-shaped peaks dominating the skyline and reflected in the hundreds of lakes and rocky pools at their feet. Lough Corrib, drained by the river Corrib, 27 miles long and 7 miles across, occupying 68 square miles of County Galway, lies in Connemara marble country, where abounds the highly polished green stone which is not really marble at all.

The twelve bens have soft-sounding names including Benbaun (2,395 feet), Bencorr (2,336 feet), Bencollaghduff (2,290 feet), Benbreen (2,276 feet), Bengower (2,184 feet) Muckanaght (2,153 feet), and Derryclare (2,220 feet). Their slopes are lichen and moss country, and Glory be! at Clifden Bay and Mannin Bay, would you believe it? there are long, long coral strands. And at Killary Bay, in County Mayo, the whole British Fleet could sail into its long fjord of over 13 fathoms deep. The county of Mayo, so poor in life-supporting landscape that it has always been called 'Mayo, God help us!', northern neighbour of County Galway, has a spectacular cliff coastline and is dominated by Croagh Patrick, St Patrick's holy mountain which rises, Vesuvius-shaped, 2,500 feet above the shores of Clew Bay. Clew Bay, 15 miles long and 6 miles wide, would take years to explore. Off the coast lies one of the most westerly islands in Europe, L-shaped Achill Island, 15 miles long by 12 miles wide, all 36,348 acres of heather and gorse with memorable mountains: Slievemore (2,204 feet), Croaghaun (2,192 feet) and Minaun (1,530 feet), plus long, sandy strands such as Keel, at the foot of the 800-foot-high

Minaun Cliffs. Croaghaun is to be approached with due caution as it drops a sheer 2,000 feet into the Atlantic without any warning.

The Carboniferous limestone landscapes of the west of Ireland make for rivers that suddenly disappear underground to as suddenly re-appear again, and thousands of secret, limestone caves beneath the rounded landscape. County Sligo, quite unexpectedly, almost suggests Swiss Alpine valleys in parts, and then rise very strange, dominating shapes such as Ben Bulben (1,730 feet); not so much a high mountain as an enormously long aircraft carrier of a limestone plateau, thrusting its way at full speed ahead for the Atlantic Ocean.

Glencar Lough, in the north of Sligo, presents a waterfall that flows upwards! This is the countryside made famous in poems by W.B. Yeats about the Lake Isle of Innisfree, of Collooney, of Dooney, of Drumcliff, of Lissadell and of Knocknarea.

Sister county to Sligo is the county of Leitrim, like Mayo, also known as 'Leitrim, God help us!', a poor land of lake and mountain with its virtually unknown mountain valleys and its towering Truskmore (2,113 feet) and Cloghcorragh (2,007 feet), and its Lough Melvin, 7½ miles long and 1½ miles wide, teeming with trout and salmon. Equally little known is Lough Allen, one of the three great Shannon lakes, 7 miles long and 3 miles wide. This part of the Shannon, at Carrick-on-Shannon, the largest river in Ireland, is now a sailing paradise with two huge, modern marinas.

The eastern boundary of County Roscommon is formed by the River Shannon as it wanders down to the rather nondescript city of Limerick and ambles on, past Shannon airport, on its way to the Atlantic coast. On the north side of the estuary of the Shannon is the county of Clare, two thirds Carboniferous limestone and one third, by the Atlantic, of Clare Shales. This is largely moonscape country, looking like the location for a modern 'Star Wars' film. Within this glacial,

gravel, one-time mass of ice is the area known as the Burren, the largest natural rock-garden in Europe, with every type of exotic wild plant and flower, and a secret playground for all types of rare moths and butterflies. The Atlantic edge of County Clare above Liscannor Bay suddenly rises to the cliffs of Moher, some 800 feet high and home of myriad wild sea birds.

Just visible from the topmost point of the fabulous cliffs of Moher 30 miles away, are the scattered, limestone-rock islands which form the world-famous Aran Islands. These are virtually a continuation of the County Clare landscape in island form, Inishmore (7,365 acres), Inishmaan (2,252 acres), and Inisheer (1,400 acres). On Inishmore (the 'capital' is Kilronan) is the half-circle fort of Dun Aengus, with its back to a sheer, 300-foot-drop into the Atlantic Ocean.

Swinging wildly away from this next outpost to America, and heading back far across the rather dreary midlands, it is well worth looking at the more civilised and prosperous landscape of the Rivers Suir, Nore and Barrow, which help to make the counties of Waterford, Tipperary and Kilkenny, on the south east coast of Ireland, so prosperous. These rivers, known as the 'three sisters', merge into the harbour of Waterford. Much of the north and centre of County Waterford is mountainous, dominated by the Comeragh Mountains, over 2,500 feet high. The coastline is impressive and attractive with tiny harbours, small peninsulas and sandy strands, such as Dunmore East, Tramore, Dungarvan, Ardmore and Cappoquin.

The valley of the Blackwater is one of the most gracious, wooded places in Ireland, at its best around Lismore. Tipperary, the 'Golden Vale' of Ireland, is a rich pastureland of limestone vales and sandstone hills. Probably the most beautiful parts of the very lovely county of Tipperary are the Galtee Mountains and the incomparably attractive Glen of Aherlow.

The Knockmealdowns, the mountain range in the north,

includes Slievenamon at 2,368 feet and Keeper Hill at 2,275 feet. In the midst of the vast limestone lowland of the Golden Vale of Tipperary, amid its cattle land and dairy farming, suddenly there appears from the limestone plain the surging, solid outcrop of the Rock of Cashel, on which is perched the Irish Acropolis, rising 200 feet above the plain.

Kilkenny is the county of Kilkenny 'marble'; not real marble but polished black Carboniferous limestone. This is a county of undulating limestone hills, and Carlow, the adjacent county, has some of the most fertile fields in Ireland, well watered by the River Barrow.

Originally one of the most prosperous counties in Ireland, Wexford presents a county with the longest and lowest sand and shingle coastline of any in Ireland. Off the coast is the European bird sanctuary of the Saltee Islands. Bird sanctuaries abound on the county's salt marshes and the land stretches out in long necks to Hook Head, Forlorn Point, Carnsore Point and Rosslare Point. Sand dunes and coastal lagoons are many, and all too often the granite Tuskar Rock claimed its victims until a lighthouse was built on top, so that now only near misses occur in the treacherous waters.

The county of Wexford slips gracefully into the county of Wicklow, the 'Garden of Ireland'. This is largely civilised parklands with wondrous valleys such as the glacial valley of Glendalough, the valley of the Avoca, and the granite highlands of the Leinster chain of mountains. This is one time gold and lead and zinc mining country. Here, the Cambrian rock of Lugnaquilla dominates the landscape above the granite Leinster Mountains of 3,039 feet in height. From the watershed of the Wicklow mountains rises the source of Dublin's River Liffey. Typical of the Wicklow scenery is the Little Sugar Loaf Mountain, looking like a mini volcano, which it is not, as it is a fold of upland only 1,120 feet high, and pleasantly walkable. The Wicklow granite landscape looks to be on a huge scale but really it is on a very minor scale, almost an ornamental Japanese landscape or Chinese garden landscape in its graciousness.

Dear, Dirty Dublin – the 'Dark Pool' – is flat, like the accents of its inhabitants. It is, for the most part, built on reclaimed slob-lands, and on post-glacial estuarial and marine deposits, and includes some fine beaches and one solid rock of the Hill of Howth.

When it comes to mixed Irish metaphors, such as 'the land where the hand of man never set foot,' then, geologically speaking, the best wine which has been kept to the last, is the wildly scenically beautiful highland of Kerry, the highland of Cork, the county that can justly claim to be the Texas of Ireland. The county of Kerry, of superlative soft beauty, is known as 'The Kingdom of Kerry', and it is just that, a kingdom of Carboniferous and Old Red Sandstone, flowing from east to west from the Carboniferous limestone and Nanurian Rocks of Cork, with its sandstone promontories.

The most spectacular county in Ireland, Kerry, has ever present the disturbing waters of the Atlantic Ocean, and is primarily a sea-county of towering mountains reflected in dazzling bays, sparkling lakes and trembling estuaries. Here are the highest mountains in the whole of Ireland, the very highest being Carrantuohill at 3,414 feet. Three of the most spectacular peninsulas are in the south-east corner of Ireland, the Old Red Sandstone heights of the Dingle Peninsula, with outposts of ancient Devonian rock emerging from a hinterland of Carboniferous rocks. Iveragh, with its Valencia Island and Skellig rocks, is almost totally Old Red Sandstone, while the third major peninsula is equally old and shot with Carboniferous rock in the forms of Bantry Bay, Dunmanus Bay and Roaring Water Bay.

For many, the Dingle Peninsula – 'Ryan's Daughter' land in film terms – has all the glamour of Mount Brandon, 3,127 feet (St Brendan's holy mountain), the second highest mountain in the county, and the spectacular Connor Pass, 1,500 feet up, and with thirty miles of wild, mountainous highland country falling headlong into the deep green and black waters of the turbulent Atlantic Ocean. Here is the stuff of which Shakespeare spoke when he wrote of the 'Cloud-capped palaces, the gorgeous towers...' It is heady, romantic scenery where the last of the great Golden Eagles of Kerry made their nests. The Blasket Islands, no longer inhabited, are seven in number, Great Blasket Island being four miles long and almost a mile wide, just off the Kerry coast.

While the highlands of Kerry are of such majestic and sweeping beauty, the Lakes of Killarney, 'Heaven's Reflex', have captured the imagination of the world. Gouged out by glaciers, these lakes, well wooded with arbutus, oak, ash, holly and birch and with lush vegetation of ferns and fuchsia, have a superb skyline which includes the Macgillycuddy's Reeks and the Purple Mountain group. The three largest lakes of Killarney are Lough Leane (the lower lake), the Torc (the middle lake) and the Upper Lake. From the heights of Aghadoe, which is like a viewing platform, the mountains fall away in the distance: Crohane (2,162 feet), Bennaunmore (1,490 feet), Stoompa (2,280 feet), Mangerton (2,750 feet), Torc (1,760 feet) and Cromaglan (1,225 feet). Giant boulders are flung about everywhere, and the Gap of Dunloe rises up in a pony path four miles long between the Macgillycuddy (pronounced Mac-lecuddy) Reeks and the Purple Mountains, rising from sea level to eight hundred feet or so.

While the Victorian system of primary education taught in its geography lessons that Ireland was shaped like a saucer, not an Irish saucer either, because nothing Irish was taught in these schools, which were very much part of the 'British Isles', the fact is that Ireland really has the shape of an oval and over-baked pigeon pie. It has an enormously high crust around the edges of varying heights and shapes, and degrees of blackness and brownness, while the middle of the pie has gently subsided into a flat, crusty middle, with occasional lumps here and there, like the soft shape of pigeon's breasts. This pie, fruit of the day's widgeon shoot, held to stop the little beggars stuffing their craws with fresh, young green peas from the kitchen gardens, has been presented on an old oval serving dish, chipped at the edges, and with cracks in its Sèvres china running from east to west.

This pigeon pie is fit to be served at a Roman feast, but the Romans never had the good fortune to land in Ireland, so they missed such a Lucullan delight. The real Irish pigeon pie is served at dinner in a damp Palladian house, where the retired colonel and his tweedy guests have shot the pigeons on the wing, very neatly through the head, so cook has no problem with any grains of lead shot in the plump bodies. (The cook, of course, served her time in the kitchens of the Vice-Regal lodge in Dublin. In the village she is well known as the 'Cordon Blue'. Her sole reading material are the books of Elizabeth David. When she goes to London on her annual visit to her sister, who served her time in the kitchens of Buck House, she takes the opportunity of watching Delia Smith cooking on telly. They don't have the telly in the Palladian house, and the pigeon pie is a unique work of art, because when the Calor gas cylinder runs out on the ancient stove it is finished off in the turf-fired oven). Geography, it is said, is about maps, while history, it is said, is about chaps, but in actual life the two subjects merge and reflect each other as is shown in the making of the Irish pigeon pie.

The geographical 'pigeon-pie' that forms the landscape of Ireland is a mixture of basalt rocks in the North, limestone in the middle, and Old Red Sandstone in the South West. Each of these basic rock formations has its own character: volcanic, placid, gentle or overbearing. The Good Lord called Peter a ' Rock', and who are we to doubt that the rock formations of Ireland do not have profound effects on the Irish people who share so many a rock formation? While the rocks took hundreds of millions of years to come about, the first people who inhabited the island of Ireland arrived there seven to eight or nine thousand years before Christ walked on the earth and the waters of the Middle East.

One of the brightest jewels in the crown of the Kingdom of Kerry is the long valley at the foot of Bentee Mountain, looking out across the estuary to Valentia Island (no longer literally an island since it was linked by a million-pound bridge to the mainland) with, just nine miles out to sea, the jagged fingers of the Skelligs rocks pointing up to the sky out of the dark depths of the Atlantic Ocean. These spectacular, cathedral-spire-like pinnacles of grey, like gigantic pieces of shrapnel, rise sheer-sided out of the frenzied seas. They are made up of the Great Skellig, the Little Skellig and Lemon Rock. As Sir Kenneth Clark, the visionary author of the television series, 'Civilisation', pointed out in the first of these programmes, the Great Skellig was an 8th century Christian monastic settlement, the remains of which still stand, despite the elements and devastating raid after raid by pagan, plundering and murdering Vikings.

Like the anchorites of the first days of Christianity, and inspired by the earliest of desert fathers, the Irish monks clung to the rock in six little beehive cells and worshipped in two tiny, stone chapels. They founded the most westerly outpost of Christianity in Europe at a time when it was plunged into darkness by the invading Norsemen and Vikings from Scandinavia who controlled the seas. On the main rock is the Chapel of Saint Michael, hence this largest of the three rocks is called 'Skellig Michael'. Ladder-like stone steps, hewn from the solid rock, lead to this earliest of western monastic centres of study and learning and prayer and worship, now inhabited by puffins and a multitude of other unusual sea birds.

The next door neighbour to the mountainous wonderland of the Kingdom of Kerry is the county of Cork. The huge county fairly ripples with folds of ancient rocks, tucked up from west to east from the county of Kerry. The long, narrow series of peninsulas in West Cork is comparatively unknown, and their originality of character is preserved. It is 'Wild West' country, with canyons and passes, curling roads and rock outcrops and masses of strewn boulders. The longest and deepest of these peninsulas are the Bay of Kenmare, separating Kerry from Cork, the Bay of Bantry, and the Bay of Dunmanus. The mountain ranges dividing Kerry from Cork include the Sheehy Mountains, nearly 2,000 feet high. Glengarriff, on Bantry Bay, is a Mediterranean land of fantastic beauty, with touches of Switzerland and the Rhine in its scenery. Just off the coast of Glengarriff is the Italianate

garden island of Garinish, or, as it is sometimes called, Illnacullin. Glengarriff is heavily wooded countryside with elms and oaks and pines and holly and yew. It is lush countryside with a profusion of hedges of fuchsia and groves of arbutus. This is because of the warm waters of the Gulf Stream lapping its shores, where even palm trees flourish, as well as luxurious grasses and hundreds of species of ferns. West Cork is a solitary world, with its vast and deep harbour of Kinsale, sheltered by the Old Head of Kinsale and leading a chain of small and picturesque harbours, such as Glandore, Schull and Ballydehob. The Mizen Head is the most south-westerly point in the whole country. Cork is well watered by its long, meandering River Lee which flows from west to east and on which the principal city of the county stands. The river rises in the Lake of Gougane Barra, a place of dark, brooding waters beneath the shadow of the mountain ranges bordering Kerry and Cork. To stand on the ridge of this mountain range at dawn, and look across to the county of Kerry, is to experience all the wonder and tranquillity of Dvorak's Largo movement in his 'New World' Symphony. Because of the ripple of Old Red Sandstone through the county there are spectacular outcrops such as Mount Gabriel, over 1,300 feet high, dominating the landscape.

The little known south coast of Cork embraces a coastline from Galley Head and the Bay of Clonakilty to Courtmacsherry Bay, and on to the vast and deep entrance to Cork Harbour which begins at Cobh, and then on to East Cork to the inlets and bays of Ballycotton and of Youghal. The entrance to Cork Harbour through the deep waters of Cobh and the River Lee leads to Cork itself, the 'marshy place', a city divided into two by the pleasant waters of the River Lee. North of Cork, and north of the River Lee, are the Boggerath Mountains, over 2,000 feet in height, and the Nagle mountains, nearly 1,500 feet high. The Blackwater River is even more beautiful than the River Lee as it meanders its way through glorious, wooded gorges. The character of Cork is much formed by its two rivers, the Lee and the Blackwater, and by its outcrop and ranges of mountains above its fertile and much watered valleys. The limestone ridges flow from west to east and the coastline, so heavily indented with deep bays and tiny, secret, offshore islands, and a hundred magic strands, make its 2,880 square miles a region of great beauty and magnificence. The Cork-Kerry mountain range border is strong stuff, heady viewing which broods in the memory for a long, long time. This huge diversity of landscape, from the Mediterranean to the Alpine to the fjord, makes for a people of great intellect, subtle speech and soft manners, and probably the influence of the mountains makes for madly romantic, born-free rebels who are great at backing lost causes and enjoying and enduring the consequences.

The climate of Ireland can be summed up by the general statement that it is moderate, in European terms, by nature of its surrounding seas. There are no great extremes of temperature, the coldest months of January and February ranging between roughly 4 and 7 degrees Celsius, while in the hottest months, June, July and August, the temperature ranges from 14 to 16 degrees Celsius. May is the sunniest month. For the whole of the country the average rainfall lies between 800mm and 1,200mm; a village in, say, southwest Kerry, for example, would experience an average of twice the annual rainfall in London. So, moist, mild and often changeable might best sum up the climate of the Emerald Isle. Snow is rare, except on high mountain tops in the winter, but the one constant climatic factor is the wild west wind. It blows almost non-stop, from the Atlantic west to the east coast, and across the flat plains of Clare or the mountains of Donegal or Kerry it whistles in at speeds varying from 60 to 80 miles per hour, and has been known to reach a speed of over 100 miles per hour. Consequently, there are few trees on the west coast, and the few huddled stunted things there are crouch with their backs to the wind and their branches bent eastwards. The Atlantic waves, aided by the winds, break into spray as high as 300 or 400 feet in some places. The high rainfall leads to lush pasturelands in 40 shades of green. High rainfall and mild waters make for luxuriant plant life and for sodden peat bogs. Sheltered coastal inlets and valleys and limestone plains lead to Mediterranean-type resorts and

plants, with some two-thirds of the land agricultural land of varying degrees of wealth, to a remaining one third of rough grazing land.

In the uplands there can be good pastoral land, and an enormous area of Ireland is prime bogland – 'peat' land. With its oak and other natural forests cleared in the 17th century, only about seven per cent of the land is under re-afforestation, mostly in young firs and pines.

The flora of Ireland is about two thirds of that of Britain, and of a smaller range than in the larger countries of Europe, yet it includes unusual Alpine-Arctic vegetation, particularly in the Burren of County Clare, and many Mediterranean plants in the counties of Sligo, Clare and Kerry. Hawthorn, blackthorn, bracken and heathers and gorse abound, and the lakelands are a paradise of rushes and sedges.

Relatively unknown are the many attractive coastal sand dunes of Ireland, and tidal salt and fresh-water marshlands and lagoons, which are all too rare in Europe, and are scenes of rare, wild bird life.

The fauna of Ireland includes 380 different species of wild birds, of which 135 breed in the country. Freshwater fish include salmon, trout, char, eel, pike and rainbow trout. There are no snakes but there is one indigenous reptile, a common lizard. In the land of amphibians there are native specimens of frog, toad and newt, and 31 species of mammals.

Because Ireland became an island before Britain, you will not find snakes or weasels or moles, and only two kinds of Irish mice. The Irish hare is a whopping great fellow, quite distinct and much larger and fleeter than his British relatives. The Irish hare, with the lovely Latin title of *Lepus timidus hibernicus*, looks foxy red and can weigh up to 7 pounds. He, or she, can be found in grasses or heather, or even in the middle of the grasses of the busy airport runways at Dublin and at Shannon. The Irish stoat *Mustela erminea hibernica* has a red and brown back with a white front. The Irish hare and the Irish stoat are unique to Ireland, as is the little known Bull Island mouse. Now extinct are the Irish elks, whose great antlered skeletons are discovered in bogs from time to time, and which disappeared off the face of Ireland about 8,000 or 9,000 B.C.

The natterjack toad, *Bufo Calamita* to amphibian experts, pops up in County Kerry and is locally referred to as the 'black frog'.

The Irish frog, a runner rather than a 'leaper', has its place in history, as the historian Giraldus Cambrensis, secretary to Henry II's son Prince John, when he visited Ireland, wrote in 1187, that there were 'neither snakes nor adders, toads nor frogs, tortoises nor scorpions nor dragons! It produces, however, spiders, leeches and lizards, but they are quite harmless. It does appear very wonderful that, when anything venemous is brought there from other lands it never could exist in Ireland'. He does, however, mention a frog found in Waterford, and brought to Court to the amazement of the people there. Whether the Irish frog was there before Prince John or appeared afterwards is a matter for debate.

When it comes to bird life, Ireland offers such diverse landscapes that it is a sanctuary for many birds which are fast disappearing from the face of Europe. What woods there are have all the usual song birds, while the curlew haunts the bogs and marshes, and herons majestically stalk the lakes and estuaries. Snipe are to be found on the moors, along with black-headed gulls and golden plovers and white-breasted geese. The western and south-western lakes are full of swans, and all kinds of duck and teal, Arctic terns, and great crested grebes. But it is in sea-birds that Ireland excels: gannets, auks, petrels and Manx shearwaters, as well as peregrines, kestrels and choughs. Winter visitors include swans from Iceland and barnacle geese from Greenland. The Wexford slob-lands are the water home of over half of the Greenland white-fronted geese of the world, most of which winter holiday in Ireland.

Ireland today, the official Tourist Board 'Ireland of the Welcomes', is a fairly treeless land, a country of a multiplicity of small farms, narrow lanes and winding roads, thick hedgerows, misleading – if any – signposts, the occasional high-walled Ascendancy estate of what Brendan Behan described as 'the Horse Protestants', the shells of burnt out 'big houses' and one-time barracks, Macedonian-smelling market-towns and Balkan-style villages, a hundred round towers, 40,000 forts, raths and 'fairy rings', and thousands of crannogs, dolmens, tumuli, stone circles and pillar stones. Gone are the dense oak forests of Elizabethan times.

The Ireland seen by the first inhabitants was an entirely different sight, almost as if it was on another planet, for it would have been just less than ten thousand years ago, when the great ice age was on the retreat, and the glaciers covering the island disappeared as the climate warmed up, that man advanced as the vegetation and animal life gave him an existence. To live then, man had to hunt and gather food. From the Europe of the greatest works of art, the cave painters of Lascaux in the Dordogne in France, and the rock painters of La Pasiega in Spain, the first inhabitants of Ireland came.

The historical evidence for the appearance of the first inhabitants comes in the form of the clues they left behind, notably their axes – flints mounted on bone or wooden shafts – and their arrows. The 'frozen' Ireland of nine or ten thousand years ago saw masses of water in its glaciers and, consequently, the sea levels were substantially different from today's, and the land bridges with Britain and France were sundered as the ice melted and formed new seas and oceans. The southern part of Ireland was the first to escape the ice barriers and there is evidence that the northern shores of Ireland were much higher than they are today.

In the mind-boggling time scale of a million-and-a-half years or so of man in Europe, 'thousands' of years in time become a matter of conjecture and debate, particularly in the history of man in Ireland. Until the 1980s the history books of Ireland dated the first inhabitants as coming in 6,000 B.C., by the shortest route to Ireland from Scotland. Now, modern research has proved that the first people living in Ireland were most certainly there by 9,000 B.C. This has come about notably by the superb scientific researches of Dr P.C. Woodman, Assistant Keeper of Antiquities at the Ulster Museum in Belfast, at Mount Sandel, on a headland looking out over the River Bann, in County Derry; by the excavations carried out by Michael Ryan, Keeper of Irish Antiquities at the National Museum in Dublin, at Lough Boora, in County Offaly; and by Swedish archaeologist Dr Juren Burenhalt and his colleagues at Carrowmore, at the foot of the mountain of Knocknarea (1,078 feet) in County Sligo. Not only was the date of the first arrivals put back a thousand years or more, but the evidence suggests that the first inhabitants came to the west coast of Ireland from France and Spain, and not by the shortest sea route to the north-east corner of Ireland, from Scotland.

Before the very recent findings of Dr Woodman, Michael Ryan and Dr Burenhalt, our knowledge of pre-historic man in Ireland was confined to the finding of 6th millennium B.C. flint implements in Larne, in County Antrim. In fact axe finding here became a Victorian pastime. Until very recently these beachcombers who had come from Scotland were the popular bet for being first arrivals in Ireland, although finds in Sutton, in County Dublin, were roughly of the same date, and of similarly roaming or nomadic beach peoples.

At Mount Sandel, in County Derry, Dr Woodman made the exciting find of what is probably the first known permanent 'house' in Europe. This took the form of a discovery of a pattern of post holes which were the remains of circular wooden huts about 6 metres across, the 20-centimetre-deep holes being set at an angle in the ground. The dome-shaped circular buildings would have been of strong saplings bent inwards and lashed together with a weatherproof covering of lighter branches woven-in, and a bank of sods around the circumference of the huts. At Mount Sandel they were hut builders and not builders of tents, and the occupants made permanent, all-the-year-round homes there, as is evidenced by the rubbish pits of the remains of food such as salmon and hazelnuts, and the remains of bones of birds such as duck, grouse and pigeon, and of hares and wild boar. The hazelnuts, their charred nut shells found in the hearths, provided the main source for the archaeologists for their radio carbon dating. This was not an isolated group of eight or ten people either, it was a regular settlement of many people. The flint tools found on the site were unknown outside Ireland. The carbon datings established beyond doubt that there was a community alive and well in Mount Sandel in the 8th millennium B.C.

In the case of Lough Boora in County Offaly, this was a lake in the centre of a large peat bog in central Ireland. When Bord na Mona, the Irish Peat Board, drained the area prior to moving in their vast machines to harvest the peat commercially to provide fuel for the State's power stations to generate electricity, another and larger lake was unearthed, beneath which was an archaeologist's dream: a hoard of pebble axes, hearths with bird, mammal and fish bones and burnt hazelnut shells, and various other artefacts.

These other artefacts were made of chert, as flint was not to be found in central Ireland. The radio-carbon datings of Lough Boora ranged from 7,000 B.C. to 6,500 B.C. Boora was probably more a temporary stopover for a nomadic group who roamed the area as the seasons changed. The ground pebble axe-heads of Lough Boora are in strong contrast to the fine flint heads found in Larne.

When Dr Juren Burenhalt of the Institute of Archaeology in Stockholm began to excavate in the west of Ireland, in County Sligo, at Carrowmore, near the mountain of Knocknorea, he found on this broad peninsula one of the biggest megalithic graveyards in Europe; some 50 sites complete with burial chambers surrounded by one ton boulders. His findings upset the theory previously held that the famed underground tombs at Newgrange on the River Boyne were the first in the country and the work of megalithic tomb builders moving across Europe from the

Mediterranean, via the English Channel and the Irish Sea, to the east coast of Ireland.

In the Carrowmore tombs are the cremated remains of hundreds of human bodies. Scientific surveys from the air showed up to 100 settlement sites in this mysterious landscape so loved by W.B. Yeats in his poetry. Post holes of tent-like huts were discovered, as well as flints and shard scrapers and arrow heads. Deer bones were found, and on the adjacent beach a vast, man-made terrace of empty oyster shells. From a study of the remains in the hearths there was evidence of cockles and mussels having been cooked, while the oysters were eaten raw. A child's bronze ring was found, as well as a glass bead from a necklace. The finds suggested the original people were hunters and gatherers rather than agriculturalists, who would have come later.

Probably the most exciting finds were the cremated bones of young women between the ages of 18 and 22, possibly sacrificial victims. The earliest dates for these strange settlements are reckoned at 7,400 B.C. The numbers and sizes of tombs suggest tribes of three or four families and a total of three or four hundred people dwelling on the peninsula, farming and making seasonal circuits throughout the area.

The probability now is that the people who built houses for their dead, and the spirits of their dead, spread from the west of Ireland to the Boyne Valley, and not the other way round.

The findings of these three archaeologists suggests that the first people to come to Ireland were set up in business by the eighth millennium, complete with weapons and tools of quite advanced 'technology', flint and stone and pebble axes and flint heads and blades, and they lived by fishing and killing birds, and on sea food and edible plants. By the 4th millenium B.C. they were settled farmers, mainly on the east coast, in the northern part of the country and on the west coast.

These were the first 'Irish' who discovered and worked the nation's natural resources and can thus be reckoned the forerunners of modern Ireland and its culture. They were the first 'Irish' to fit into the Irish landscapes, and to regard them as their permanent home.

History is nothing if it is not about ordinary people, how they lived and loved and how they died. It is not really about High Kings and Princes of the Church, these values being rather the product of Victorian historical teaching, so that we might all 'Bless the squire, and his relations, and keep us in our proper stations'. It is sad, therefore, that we know little or nothing, as yet, about the living people of so long ago who built such magnificent tombs to house their dead in the mountains of Sligo and elsewhere; a polished stone axe here, some bird bones and fish bones, and flint instruments there, and some fragments of beakers or pottery; these are all the signs we have left of the living.

However, as the tombs of the dead gained in size and magnificence, and began to be given their first primitive, artistic decorations, so the numbers of people living in Ireland must have increased considerably to have raised so many stones of such enormous size. From the sea-edge and the estuaries the first people made clearings in the forests and moved into primitive huts as they tended their goats and sheep and cattle and planted their barley and wheat. The 'Megalithic' man, meaning literally the age of the men of 'great stones', saw hundreds upon hundreds of megalithic tombs rising throughout Ireland. The first were the court cairns, long burial chambers surmounted by large stones placed on top of the mounds and surrounded by tall standing stones. Then came the mysterious passage-graves, such as those in the valley of the Boyne, when extraordinary eastern and reptilean spirals and curves began to appear on the entrance stones and on the stone passages within, along with sun rays, triangles and zigzags and simple line drawings of the human face and figure. Since the same artistic motifs are common to Brittany and to Portugal, it is not unreasonable to assume that these artists and builders came from the Iberian Peninsula.

The most common form of prehistoric burial seen in Ireland is the portal dolmen, that is the sort of enormous stone table made up of a huge capstone, often triangular, supported by three or four large standing stones. They occur regularly on the east coast, and in many cases the capstone weighs one hundred tons. After this came the Bronze Age with its gallans or standing stones, and the Iron Age with its series of hill-forts and ring-forts, and crannogs, the latter often being in the middle of a lake, or on a peninsula.

Most beautiful of all stone decorations are those swirling motifs at the entrance to the great burial places of Newgrange, Dowth and Knowth, in the valley of the Boyne. Some experts link these intricate spirals and diamond and lozenge shapes directly with the Far East, and particularly with the continent of India. This falls in line with the findings of experts such as Professor Myles Dillon, who held that the Irish language had similar roots to Sanskrit, and therefore had links with India and its civilisation, and who is to say that his theory is not correct?

Newgrange is of particular importance historically, as it may well have housed a primitive astronomical observatory. Some carvings suggest a tracing of lunar movements, but what is certain and most extraordinary is that the builders of the Newgrange tomb knew all about the summer and winter solstice, enabling them to calendar the planting of their crops. If you stand in the centre of the tomb at Newgrange on the shortest day of the year, in the month of December, and draw an imaginary line to the very edge of the mound, and to the far horizon, the rays of the rising sun strike through a tiny aperture above the main entrance and fill the interior with light along this line for the first twenty minutes or so of the day. This cannot be mere coincidence. The builders must have known precisely what they were doing, either for the purpose of sacrificial sun-worship, or purely for measuring the start of the agricultural season.

With the Bronze Age came Ireland's golden age of magnificently-worked gold objects and collars and ornaments of intricate craftsmanship. With this gold period came also a time of the making of bronze shields, trumpets, pots, buckets and cauldrons. Much of the later gold ornamentation bore all the hallmarks of the Celtic La Tène style in art, which was the peak of artistic achievement throughout Europe in these centuries before Christ. This unique curvilinear Celtic motif style proves that the La Tène Celts must have been flourishing in Ireland at least one hundred years before the birth of Christ and, for the first time, one can really begin to call the inhabitants of the island 'Celts'. Arguably the most outstanding example of La Tène art in Ireland is the granite Turoe Stone in a field at Turoe House, three-and-a-half miles north of the market-town of Loughrea in County Galway. The Turoe Stone was actually found at the ring fort of Feerwore. It is an enormous, dome-topped stone with curvilinear designs in flowing spirals and elliptical decorations, about four feet in height. It is pure La Tène in period and scholars are at a loss to explain its true significance. It has every appearance of being associated with a Celtic pagan cult or religion. What few Irish archaeologists or historians are prepared to admit in public is that it is quite frankly phallic and in all probability was part of some obscure fertility cult or rite, but who really knows or who is going to admit it?

From this time on, about 500 B.C., one can begin to talk of landscapes inhabited by a Celtic people who spoke the Celtic language and were part of that vast culture which was the Europe before the real 'barbarians', the Romans, came and smashed it to pieces, with the exception of Ireland whereon no conquering Roman foot has ever trod. Again, because of a written language, Latin, the Romans have been given pride of place in history, while the Celts, who had only an oral tradition, have been much underestimated culturally and aesthetically, and demoted historically. It is only in comparatively recent years that the true nature of the magnificent culture of the Celts is coming to light, too long obscured by the elaborate Roman historical overlay of obscurity and lack of comprehension.

The heydays of the Celts were probably from the eighth century B.C. through until Roman times, and again after the fall of the Roman Empire. The Celtic people stretched from Ireland through Britain and across Europe as far as Greece and Turkey. In fact, when St Paul was preaching to the Galatians he was actually preaching to Celts. The Celts, in itself a Greek word, were the original inhabitants of what we now know as the cities of Paris, Budapest and Belgrade.

Ireland in the years around 800 B.C. was a part of the Celtic Hallstatt culture which continued throughout Europe until about 400 B.C. This earliest form of Celtic culture is so named because it was first identified on the shores of Lake Hallstatt, in Austria, where exciting Celtic finds were made during archaeological excavations in 1846. This period of Celtic culture was followed by the La Tène culture, named for important finds made in 1858 in La Tène in Switzerland, on the banks of the River Thielle, flowing into Lake Neuchâtel. This culture lasted until the coming of the Romans and survived, notably in Ireland, when the Celts constantly raided the Romans retreating from the shores of Britain and of Europe on the fall of their Empire.

The incisive G.K. Chesterton put his finger on the Celtic temperament when he wrote:

'The Great Gaels of Ireland
Were the men whom God made mad,
For all their wars were merry
And all their songs were sad.'

To the Victorian Young Irelanders, like the poet Thomas D'Arcy McGee, the Celts were seen through madly romantic, rose-tinted spectacles when, for example, he wrote, in the poem 'The Celts',

'Long, long ago, beyond the misty space
of twice a thousand years,
In Erin old there dwelt a mighty race
Taller than Roman spears...'

The probability is rather that they were short, hairy little men, mad about war, who went into battle almost naked but for bronze helmet and belt, and possibly a decorative torque around the neck.

One of the best descriptions of G.K. Chesterton's 'Great Gaels' is that of Diodorus Siculus, a Roman historian of the first century before Christ, who wrote:

'Physically the Celts are terrifying in appearance, with deep-sounding and very harsh voices. In conversation they use few words and speak in riddles, for the most part hinting at things and leaving a great deal to be understood. They frequently exaggerate with the aim of extolling themselves and diminishing the status of others. They are boasters and threateners and given to bombastic self-dramatization, and yet they are quick of mind and with good natural ability for learning.'

Anybody listening to the conversation of an Irishman today in a Dublin snug, Brooklyn bar or Kilburn pub would not find much to quarrel with in this Roman appraisal written one hundred years or so before the birth of Christ.

Anybody brought up on a Classical or semi-Classical diet of Latin and Greek will be thoroughly versed in the affairs of the Roman writers, historians and soldier-politicians such as Julius Caesar. Few among them are unaware of the fact that Caesar divided the Celts of Gaul into three parts and smashed their Celtic civilisation when he finally defeated their chieftain Vercingetorix at the Battle of Alesia. Only in recent times have the French restored some of their former Celtic glory, and their national sense of humour in the writings of Goscinny, illustrated by Uderzo, in the adventures of the Gallic hero Asterix, who – with the strength of the magic potion brewed by the druid Getafix, and the support of his companions, the wild-boar-eating Obelix, with the music of the bard, Cacofonix, and the bravery of the chief of his tribe, Vitalstatistix – kept one spot in Gaul free from the Roman legionaries led by Platypus the centurion, Convolvulus the strategist, and Magnumopus.

The humour of Goscinny and Uderzo is only matched by the legendary cartoons in *Punch*, of Roman soldiers, one of the most notable cartoons being that of two legionaries on a beach in Gaul, who have just received their shots in the arm from the medical officer, and one soldier remarks to the other 'Anti-flu, it must be Britain!'

Without written records, only an oral tradition of history, the Celts of Ireland and France and elsewhere in Europe have not fared well. We have only the biased, written word of their adversaries and conquerors, the Romans, to speak for them. Napoleon III, who was a keen archaeologist, helped his nation to unearth thousand upon thousand of Celtic burial mounds, particularly in the Champagne district of France. In many of these graves the warriors were buried in their chariots with their flagons at their feet and their swords in their iron scabbards. The warriors had lain in their tombs since the days of the various La Tène cultures, from 500 B.C. to 50 B.C. Like their confrères in Sligo and elsewhere in Ireland the manner of their funeral rites still remains virtually unknown, as do their one-eyed pagan gods and their druidic rites, long since lost and buried in former oak forests and secret graves.

The difference between Gaul and Britain and Ireland was that no conquering Roman foot ever trod upon Irish soil. The legionary SPQR banner was never planted in triumph after a major battle on Irish land. There were no straight Roman roads laid down in Ireland, no forts, no villas, no centrally-heated houses, no bath-houses or Roman brothels. Roman 'law and order', the law and order which reigns in the graveyard, never touched the hearts or minds of the Celtic-Irish people. They watched, and they saw their chance to help in the pulling down of Roman Britain, and they came back to Ireland from their sea raids with slaves and booty.

Because the Celts did not have a spoken language which the Greeks and the Romans could comprehend, to them it sounded like 'bar-bar-bar', the sound of 'barbarians', and because there was no written language, they were not regarded as civilised.

Aristotle, the Greek philosopher, writing in 330 B.C. said of the Celts:

'We have no word for the man who is excessively fearless; perhaps one may call such a man mad or bereft of feelings, who fears nothing, neither earthquakes nor waves, as they say of the Celts. It is not bravery to withstand fearful things through ignorance, for example, if through madness one were to withstand the onset of thunderbolts, and again, even if one understands how great the danger is, it is not bravery to withstand it through high-spiritedness, as when the Celts take up arms to attack the waves, and in general the courage of barbarians is compounded with high-spiritedness'.

Said Strabo, the Greek geographer of the last century B.C. and the first century A.D.:

'The whole race, which is now called Gallic or Galatic, is madly fond of war, high-spirited and quick to battle, but otherwise straightforward and not of evil character. And so, when they are stirred up they assemble in their bands for battle, quite openly and without forethought, so that they are easily handled by those who desire to outwit them; for at any time or place or on whatever pretext you stir them up, you will have them ready to face danger, even if they have nothing on their side but their own strength and courage.'

From Cornelius Tacitus, A.D. 56 to A.D. 115, the Roman senator and historian, in his 'Agricola', and also in his 'Germania', we have a brilliant picture of the Celts, particularly as seen through the eyes of his father-in-law, Julius Agricola, who governed Britain from A.D. 78 to A.D. 84. Tacitus was typical of the 'civilised' Romans in as much as he was a friend of Pliny the Younger, but, like all 'civilised' Roman intellectuals and men of letters of his time, he kept his head down in order to save it under the tyrannical regimes and abominations of Nero and Domitian. Like most Roman Classical writers he was not all that accurate in his history, and woefully ignorant in his geography, but his writing had 'style'. Tacitus had a vague notion that Ireland lay between

Spain and Britain. His father-in-law Agricola conquered most of Britain, and got as far as Anglesey in Wales, in his Welsh campaign, and as far as Ayrshire in occupying Scotland. It was while he was in Scotland, in A.D. 82, that he peered cautiously across the narrow sea to Ireland and considered invading it. Like many career generals down the ages until the present day, he vastly underestimated his proposed adversary. In his military vanity he thought that one Roman Legion, about five-and-a-half-thousand trained troops, and a back up of auxiliaries, would have been a sufficient force to invade and conquer the whole of Ireland.

Tacitus writes of Ireland:

'Agricola started his fifth campaign by crossing the river Arran, and in a series of successful actions vanquished nations hitherto unknown. The side of Britain that faces Ireland was lined with his forces. His motive was rather hope than fear. Ireland, lying between Britain and Spain, and easily accessible also from the Gallic sea, might serve as a very valuable link between the provinces making up the strongest part of the empire. It is small in comparison with Britain, but larger than the islands of the Mediterranean. In soil and climate, and in character and civilization of its inhabitants, it is much like Britain, and its approaches and harbours have now become better known from merchants who trade there. An Irish prince, expelled from his home by a rebellion, was welcomed by Agricola, who held him, nominally as a friend, in the hope of being able to use him. I have often heard Agricola say that Ireland could be reduced and held by a single legion with a fair-sized force of auxiliaries, and that it would be easier to hold Britain if it were completely surrounded by Roman armies, so that liberty was banished from its sight.'

Philosophically Tacitus points out, in his 'Agricola', that in due course by the 'civilising' process of the Romans in Britain 'the population was gradually led into the demoralizing temptation of arcades, baths, and sumptuous banquets. The unsuspecting Britons spoke of such novelties as "civilization," when in fact they were only a feature of their enslavement.' Meanwhile, the Celts across the water looked on in wonder, and had no chance of learning the Latin language and adopting the Latin Toga Virilis. The Romans held sway over the seas surrounding Britain, and they were utterly ruthless and without pity in warfare, and at their worst as an occupying power.

One of the more commonly accepted forms of the word 'Ireland' today, and with different meanings, is the word 'Eire', used by the Irish government to denote its jurisdiction over all the 32 counties of the Emerald Isle. The British government and its government of Northern Ireland use the word 'Eire' to denote the political entity that is the 26 counties today. Originally 'Eire' came from the Old Irish word for Ireland, all of Ireland, and in turn the word was related to the Greek word *Ierne*. At the time Britain was referred to by the Greek word Albion. Some 600 years B.C. traders from the Mediterranean, from Gaul and the Iberian peninsula, knew Ierne, and Greek geographers of the time referred to Ierne and Albion as the 'Pretanic' islands. As late as the second century A.D. the Greek geographer Ptolemy had Ireland firmly on his map of the known world. The Romans believed the 'Ultima Thule' to be beyond the island of Ireland, and presumably, if that final land was passed, you fell off the edge of the world.

Separated from Roman Britain, the Irish Celts were spared that peculiar fate suffered by Britain, once commented on by the eminent historian A.J.P. Taylor, namely that the ancient Britons and their Roman masters must have suffered from perpetual holes in their trouser or tunic pockets, such is the scattering of Roman coins by the fist-full all over the British landscape. No such finds are to be had in the bogs and fields of Ireland, but, very occasionally, Roman coins or fragments of Roman silver ornaments have been found at ancient burial sites, obviously loot brought back from Britain by Irish raiders. The Celts were generally more realistic in their booty; they brought back slaves, young girls and boys, forced into a lifetime of captivity to tend sheep and swine and cattle, who were worth their weight in gold.

The Celtic way of life in Ireland was a way of life totally and utterly different in language and manner from that of Britain. Under the Roman yoke the ancient Britons were given the slight veneer of a decadent culture. Ireland went its separate way, so that by the time the first Christian missionaries planted the Cross on Irish soil, they found a people with a highly civilised way of life with a hierarchy of kings and queens and princes, a sophisticated rule of law, and a land of learned men, poets, artists, aristocrats and druidic priests with unearthly magic and power. Speaking their own Irish language, this warrior race had a reputation for cattle raiding, human head hunting and fierce drinking. The Greeks and the Romans greatly feared the warrior race of Celts, particularly their manic disposition when inflamed by drink. The Greek and Roman writers had admiration for the men and women of the Celtic race and described them in enraptured tones as men and women of enormous stature and presence, Nordic warriors with blond hair and blue eyes, or red-heads, or shaggy-maned fighters with huge moustachios.

The Irish way of life was tribal, with an array of petty kings with annual consultative councils. The royals ruled and were free, as was the ruling caste of freemen. The masses were slaves. The priest caste of the druids had great influence as they were magicians who led and advised their people in battle. As Strabo wrote of the Celts, 'the whole race is war-mad, high-spirited and quick to do battle'. A battle was a tumultuous, chaotic affair of trumpets and horns and war cries and naked warriors fighting with total indifference to death. Frequently, battles were settled by single combat in front of assembled ranks of warriors. Chariots and horsemen added to the confusion of battle, which was based on a complete lack of discipline and order, and a high degree of individual decision making. Rather like the riot police of today drumming their shields with their batons to instil fear in their opponents, the Celts used their shields as sounding boards to increase the volume of their battle cries.

The beliefs of the superstitious Celts were mysterious and frightening. They were profoundly moved by living spirits they saw in the elements of fire, earth, water and air, and they made for themselves gods of the sea, the trees, the rocks, the rivers and the skies. Later, they half heard the myths of the gods of Greece and of Rome, and gave them an Irish setting. The druids, their priests, played on their deep superstitions and controlled the worship of the elements, officiated at bloody human sacrifices, steeped themselves in the supernatural, and gave themselves a monopoly on healing, law-making, the education of youth, and spoke as prophets and seers. They were the supreme magicians of their time, and their magic outdid any other form of witchcraft or manipulation of the occult anywhere else in the world.

Their gods were obscure and infernal gods and had their roots in the Mediterranean and the Far East. Under the influence of the far-off Romans, the Irish began to fashion crude-looking gods in stone, many of them three-faced, such as that found at Corleck, in County Cavan.

The gods came in threes. Three was a sacred and all-powerful number. Consequently, when Christianity finally made its appearance in Ireland the people had not the slightest difficulty in believing in the sacred mystery of the Holy and undivided Trinity. Place yourself on the plain of Moytura in the county of Sligo, as the sun goes down, or rises, or shines, on this most ancient of Ireland's battlefields, and you will hear the clash of arms, the neighing of horses, the rumble of chariots, the shouts of men and the roar of trumpets, and you will have no difficulty at all in believing in all the strange gods the early Celts put before themselves to worship. The triad was a common factor. A chieftain went into battle with two slaves; there were three female goddesses of war, Macha, Mórrigán and Bodb. There were three goddesses named Brigid. Dagda was the father of all the gods; a giant warrior with a huge club and a magic cauldron. Mannanán mac Liv was god of the sea, Lug was the god of light, Ogma of speech, Angus of love. Taranis was the god of thunder. Lug had the most important feast day in the calendar, the first of August. The old year ended on the feast of Samain, the first of November, which marked the dark side of the year. On the feast of Beltine, the first of May, the year of light began. Of all these deities Mórrigán was in all probability the mother-goddess, the goddess of fertility, and the most venerated.

Unlike the mythology of Greece and Rome, Irish mythology reached wild excesses of fantasy and magic, as in the mythological cycles of 'The Wooing of Etain' and 'The Battle of Moytura', followed by the 'Cuchulain' cycle, and the 'Fenian' or 'Ossianic' cycle.

Gazing out over the landscape of the plain of Moytura, it is easy to believe in the Fir Bolg, who were overcome in battle by the Tuatha De Danann – the 'People of the Goddess Dann'. They brought with them to Ireland the magic cauldron of Dagda, the spear of Lug, the sword of Nuadu, and the stone of Fál. It is easy to accept that Nuadu lost his hand in battle, and that the god of healing, Dian Cécht, fitted him out with a silver hand, and that Lug slew Balor of the Evil Eye, the one-eyed god, the sun-god with his thunderbolt. This mythical battle on the plain of Moytura, with armies rising out of the boulders and bracken and trees, with the druids curing the wounded and warriors being killed by magic spears, is a symbol of the victory of light over darkness. In their turn the Tuatha Dé Danann were defeated, and to this day they work the land under Ireland. In the long term it was inevitable that Brigid, all three, merged in the Saint Brigid of Kildare, and that the gods of the elements merged with God the Father, God the Son, and the Holy Ghost, in the Holy, undivided Trinity of Christianity.

Padraig Pearse, the Irish poet and revolutionary, writing on the destiny and future of the Gael, said this of what he called 'the bequest of our hero-sires of old':

'The Gael, like all the Celts, is distinguished by an intense and passionate love for nature. The Gael is the high-priest of nature. He loves nature, not merely as something grand and beautiful and wonderful, but as something possessing a mystic connection with and influence over man.

'In the cry of the seagull as he winged his solitary flight over the Atlantic waves: in the shriek of the eagle as he wheeled around the heights of the Kerry Mountains: in the note of the throstle as he sang his evening lay in the woods of Slieve Grot: in the roar of the cataract as it foamed and splashed down the rocky ravine: in the sob of the ocean as it beat unceasingly against the cliffs of Achill: in the sigh of the wind as it moved, ghostlike, through the oaks of Derrybawn – in all these sounds the ancient Gael heard a music unheard by other men.

'All these sounds spoke to his inmost heart in whispers mysterious and but half understood: they spoke to him as the voices of his ancestors, urging him to be noble and true – as the voices of the glorious dead calling to him across the waters from Tir-na-nOg...

'The sea, with its mighty thunderings, and its mysterious whisperings: the blue sky of day: the dark and solemn canopy of night spangled with myriad stars: the mountains and hills steeped in the magic of poetry and romance... the hero – memories of the past.'

What has been accepted as myth and legend, as for example in the case of the battles on the plains of Moytura in County Sligo, was in most cases a close parallel to actual history. It is believed that the first real Celts, as such, arrived in the Pretanic Island of Ireland and were fully in occupation of the entire island by at least 500 B.C. They were followed in 300 B.C. by the Laginians, who occupied the provinces of Leinster and Connacht, and who gave their name to the ancient province of Leinster. The Ulaid ruled the province of Ulster, and the province of Munster came into being. The last Celtic invaders of Ireland were the Gaels, or Goidels, and language experts tell us that they brought with them the Celtic tongue which is the basis of the Gaelic language, and what is also the foundation for modern, present-day spoken and written Irish. These Goidels were the occupiers of the ancient province of Munster. The whole pagan people of Ireland, of Ulster, Munster, Leinster and Connacht were attuned to the deep undertones of the mysteries of the elements, waiting, watching, listening, and observing world events, and they were at the same time actively participating in the break-up of the Roman Empire in the adjacent island, and in massive pirate sweeps up the English Channel, attacking coastal Gaul.

Through their raiding and trading throughout Europe, the Irish must have heard of the Star in the East, and of the fate of the Nazarene, Jesus Christ, nailed naked to a tree by his Roman captors, his side pierced by a Roman lance. They would have shared, too, in the darkness over the earth attendant on his death, and would have wondered. They would have had supreme contempt for the compromising Roman Governor, Pontius Pilate; for his washing his hands of the whole affair of the arrest, torture and murder of the quiet Christ-man. The civilised Celt must have heard as supreme magic of the Resurrection of Christ. Far-away happenings such as the destruction of the Temple of Jerusalem in A.D. 70 would have percolated through to their council tables, and they would have wondered as they heard of the action of the Roman general Titus, son of the Emperor Vespasian, driving a plough across the spot where once had stood the world famous Temple of Jerusalem. They would have heard, too, of the victory Triumph when Jewish captives were led through the streets of Rome, and the building of the Triumphal Arch of Titus which is still standing in Rome today. Too often Celtic captives in chains had, themselves, appeared in these triumphant and degrading Roman spectacles.

Because of its most westerly geographical position off the land-mass of Europe, Ireland was the last nation in that direction to receive the message of Christ. So it was not until the 5th century that Christianity, and its attendant Graeco-Roman culture, hit the Irish people. The question arises as to whether the Roman Bishop Palladius or the West Briton Patrick was the first Christian missionary to the Irish. On this vital historic matter there was, at one time, a quite mischievous theory floated by the eccentric Professor Alfie O'Rahilly, President of University College Cork, that there

had been, in fact, two Saint Patricks. He claimed that Palladius had also been known by his second name, 'Patricius', and was the first Patrick, followed in his mission by the second Patrick, the West Briton, who continued the earlier missionary work. The Saint Patrick of legend and popular belief, Professor Alfie O'Rahilly claimed, was a mixture of the two real-life Patricks. In this theory he had the support of some members of the Dublin Institute for Advanced Studies (much parodied in undergraduate rags as the 'Bored of Higher Studies'), which had been set up with the aid of one of Ireland's greatest intellectuals of all time, Eamonn De Valera. A mathematician of genius, he was one of the very few academics in Ireland who understood Einstein's Theory of Relativity. Professor Alfie O'Rahilly set out his Patrician theory in 1942. He was an academic of extraordinary diversity of talents who collected doctorates like some people collect beer mats.

To understand the mind of a man who could dream up two Saint Patricks it is worth looking at his life. There were in fact two O'Rahillys. The first was the professor. Professor Alfie O'Rahilly the Kerryman, educated at Blackrock College in Dublin, conducted by the Holy Ghost Fathers, who tried his vocation as a Jesuit, but gave it up for an academic career at University College Cork. Jailed during the 1920 'Troubles', he then supported the new 'Free State', spent a spell in Harvard, and became President of University College Cork, where he established a reputation as a brilliant, but eccentric, professor. He ordered, for example, that all female undergraduates should wear silk stockings, and bare legs were forbidden. He was one of the very few Irishmen ever to receive all seven sacraments of the Roman Catholic Church as, after the death of his wife, he returned to his old Alma Mater, Blackrock College, Dublin, and was ordained to the Catholic priesthood for the Archdiocese of Nairobi in Kenya in 1955.

The second O'Rahilly was a Monsignor in the Roman Catholic Church in Ireland, and was a close confidant of one of the most conservative Archbishops of Dublin that the city has ever known, John Charles McQuaid, originally a Holy Ghost priest of Blackrock College, Dublin, who ordained O'Rahilly. Monsignor Alfie O'Rahilly died in 1969, after fourteen years of life as a Catholic priest. Most of his contemporaries reckoned him to be too clever by half. Most of the undergraduates who had had the benefit of his great learning reckoned that his theory of the two Saint Patricks was being too clever once too often.

Would that all professors of history, particularly Irish professors, had the enormous learning and sense of humour of one of the most remarkable of British historians of our time, A.J.P. Taylor, who could write of the Romans of Celtic times in the following learned yet light-hearted manner:

'For nearly four hundred years Celtic Britain was a province of the Roman Empire – ruled by Roman governors, administered by Roman officials, garrisoned by Roman troops, most of whom were drawn from the eastern Mediterranean. The Romans introduced all their civilised habits – metalled roads, baths, temples, courts of justice, postmen and tax collectors, gladiatorial games. What happened to the indigenous population is less clear, though they re-emerged unscathed at the end. But for some centuries Britain must have looked as Roman as Rhodesia looked English.

'The most memorable characteristic of the Romans is remarked on by few authorities. This was inveterate carelessness with their money. Fortunately they had no paper money and no banking system such as ours. They relied almost entirely on metal coins and these they dropped all over the place: at home, in the streets, on building sites, in the temples and while taking a sauna or a Turkish bath. A citizen with a purseful of coins left it in the cellar or buried it in the garden, after which he forgot about it.

'I wish I knew why the Romans behaved in this casual way. Were they so rich that they could play ducks and drakes with their money? Were there no pockets in their trousers (or rather shorts) or did the pockets have holes in them? We shall never know. At all events this plethora of lost coins has saved Roman Britain from oblivion. The coins provide historians with a pretty accurate chronology for most of the period. Hence something like a coherent history of Roman Britain can be written – indeed, knowing the unreliability of many dates, I suspect too coherently.'

And again, the penetrating comments on the Romans of the master of living English historians:

'I add two comments on Roman Britain. To read all available accounts you might suppose that the Celts ceased to exist. In fact they seem to have gone underground metaphorically. They abandoned their artistic motifs for the Roman ones throughout the Roman period and resumed their own motifs the moment the Romans had gone. Their language has few signs of Latin infiltration. Most strangely of all, Christianity flourished best in Ireland, which the Romans never conquered nor even tried to. Britain would have done much better if the Romans had kept out.

'To my mind the Romans were both boring and brutal. Their triumphs resembled the Nazi rallies at Nuremberg. Their favourite sport was to watch men killing one another or being torn to pieces by wild animals. Their religion was a jumble of rubbish. As to their language, with the verbs in the wrong place and its obsession with tables, masters and love, it can only have been devised as a form of mental torture.'

More precious than the most valuable book in the world, the wonder that is the Book of Kells, in the library of the College of the Holy and undivided Trinity in Dublin, is the Book of Armagh, the greatest single source of our knowledge of the greatest missionary in history, the West Briton, Saint Patrick. The Book of Armagh, written 1,178 years ago by the scribe Ferdomach of Armagh, is in Latin, in a firm, handwritten script as clear and as readable as any letter which comes through your letter-box today. It is a small, square volume, written on vellum.

In addition to Ferdomach, we have the life of Saint Patrick by Muirchú, written in A.D. 699, and the *Breviarium* of Tírechán, written at an earlier period, around A.D. 657. From these we have Saint Patrick's own writings, his *Confession*, and his *Epistle against Coroticus*, and we are able to judge from these just what sort of man he was, and something of his history. It is apparent from these pages that he is a figure as historical as Jesus Christ or Winston Churchill. My studies of the Saint over many years suggest that he came from the Roman city of Caerwent, in modern Gwent, which was raided many times in the 4th century by Irish pirates in search of slaves.

Saint Patrick's *Epistle to Coroticus* is a letter of grief and white-hot anger, denouncing the Welsh chief Coroticus and his soldiers, who had fallen on a defenceless band of youths and maidens the day after their public baptism, many still being in their white baptismal robes, to be either slaughtered in cold blood, or carried off to the slave markets and brothels of Europe.

From the Saint's *Confession* we have a picture of a man of enormous humility, of no great formal education, but a man who lived and led a life of total and intense prayer. We see an almost visible surrounding of himself by Christ in his famous hymn, 'St Patrick's Breastplate', sometimes known as 'The Deer's Cry', which concludes with the lines:

'Christ with me, Christ before me, Christ behind me,
Christ in me, Christ beneath me, Christ above me,
Christ on my right, Christ on my left,
Christ when I lie down, Christ when I sit down, Christ when I
    arise,
Christ in the heart of every man who thinks of me,
Christ in the mouth of every one who speaks of me,
Christ in every eye that sees me,
Christ in every ear that hears me.

I arise today
Through a mighty strength, the invocation of the Trinity,
Through belief in the threeness,

Through the confession of the oneness
of the Creator of Creation.'
(From the translation of Kuno Meyer).

Saint Patrick was certainly not an Irishman, and he had that great British virtue of tenacity of purpose which helped him to convert to Christianity the last remaining nation of pagan Celts in Europe. We know from his *Confession* that he was snatched away from his family by Irish raiders at the age of 16 and spent 6 years as a slave, herding swine on the slopes of Slemish, which was near what we call the town of Ballymena today, in County Antrim. He lived a lonely and terrifying life, but a life of profound and continuous prayer for those 6 years, and then escaped to Gaul. He had what we call a 'mature' or 'late' vocation, studied for the priesthood and then returned to Ireland as a Missionary Bishop in A.D. 432.

His coming to Ireland was symbolised by his striking of the first Paschal Fire on the hill of Slane, and breaking the total blackness decreed by the pagan High King of Tara. He took on the druids and destroyed their idols. He set up no less than 365 churches, fasted for 40 days and 40 nights in Lent, on Croagh Patrick, and converted an entire nation. This he did because, like Saint Paul, he was totally Christ-centred, and lived a life inspired by an abundance of the grace of the Holy Spirit. The Trinity was his life and his message.

Bishop Fulton Sheen said on the occasion of the celebration of the Patrician Year, in Dublin in 1961 – 'Every nation has its flower, and the shamrock Saint Patrick used in order to indicate the Trinity is reflected in the Irish people... When hate has gone out of the world, those hands which were nailed by it will detach themselves and fold together, not in judgement, but in embrace, that all the world may know how sweet is the love of the Father, the Son, and the Holy Spirit.'

We have a very good idea of Saint Patrick's travels in Ireland and where he founded his churches. Today, we can follow in his footsteps, largely due to his biographers, Muirchú and Tírecháń. Saint Patrick's second landing, (his first had been as a captive slave in the North of Ireland), was at Wicklow, at the mouth of the Vartry River. He then sailed up the east coast of Ireland, and anchored in Malahide Bay in north County Dublin. He went fishing in the estuary at Laytown, and failing to catch any fish laid a curse on the river there. He then sailed between Lambay and Lusk, and landed at Saint Patrick's Island, where you can see his footprint on the rock there today. This is just off Skerries, where he put in for water. While ashore in Skerries the locals stole his goat and killed and ate it. To this day their gentle neighbours in Rush call the men of Skerries the 'skin the goats'. Saint Patrick then sailed on along the coast, past the mountains of Mourne, to call on his old pagan slave-master at Slemish, and set up a church at Saul. He visited what is now called Downpatrick, and founded a church at Slane in County Meath after lighting the Paschal Fire there and routing the pagan druids at the royal court of Tara. Later he was to establish a church at Trim. Skerries was the scene of his missionary work, as the parish of Holmpatrick testifies today. He spent much of his missionary time around Gormanstown, Donnycarney, Drogheda, Navan, Slane and Portmarnock. He certainly visited Dublin, as Saint Patrick's Well, just inside the railings of Trinity College Dublin, at the junction of Nassau Street and Dawson Street, demonstrates to this day.

He built a church at Kells in County Meath, and at Derrypatrick, and at Ratoath. In County Westmeath he set up places of worship at Clonmellon, Clonarney and Moyashel. He laboured in the centre of Ireland, at Athlone, and in Mullingar and then visited Longford and Counties Cavan and Leitrim. He crossed the Shannon at Drumsna, near Carrick-on-Shannon, and founded a church at Kilmore. Half a dozen churches were set up in Sligo, and he journeyed through Boyle and Rosconnon as far as Westport in County Mayo. Clew Bay and Castlebar fell to his preaching and, of course, he spent a spectacular 40 days and 40 nights fasting for Lent on Chroagh Patrick. He journeyed along the coast to Killala and founded a church at Easky and a scattering of churches at Aghanagh, Shancough, Drumlease and Donaghmore.

Into Donegal via Bundoran, he set up chapels at Kildoney and at Racoo, and moved from Ballyshannon, through the Barnesmore Gap to Raphoe, setting up a church at Inishowen. In Donegal and Tyrone he set up seven churches, including those at Lettershandoney, Ardmore, Donaghedy and Badoney. Churches followed at Coleraine, Bushmills, and Giant's Causeway. He went on to establish churches in Derry and in Armagh.

Leinster saw him founding churches near Kilcock in County Kildare, and near Naas, and at Kilcullen, and in Carlow and Kilkenny. At Cashel he converted the High King and his sons, and swept through Tipperary, Limerick and Offaly. Places such as Ard Patrick clearly show the association with the saint. He is said to have founded 365 churches during his lifetime, of which we can locate about 100 today.

As for Corkmen, Kerrymen and the men of Waterford, they never had the pleasure of shaking him by the hand. Kerrymen, of course, claim that that was not necessary, as they had already been converted to Christianity by his predecessor, Bishop Palladius Patricius in A.D. 431.

To get to know the real personality of Saint Patrick is a simple matter of reading his own writings, his *Confession* and his *Epistle to Coroticus*. Anyone with the slightest knowledge of Latin can see at a glance, as the great Bollandiste scholar, Paul Grosjean points out, that Saint Patrick's Latin is not Classical written Latin but spoken Latin, spontaneous and on the spur of the moment. He was very conscious of the fact that he was no Classical scholar and in his humility he says:

'What I had to say had to be translated into a tongue foreign to me, as can be easily proved by the savour of my writing, which betrays how little instruction and training I have had in the art of words.'

Saint Patrick was a born orator and he preached in simple and powerful Latin, mainly because his Irish, picked up during his captivity in Slemish, was rough and ready and not cultured enough to match that of the perfectly cultured Irish of the Kings and Queens and Princes at whom he was aiming his Christian message, so he used Irish interpreters for his Latin preaching.

Word of mouth history, passed on down through the troubled ages when the spoken word, the oral tradition, was pre-eminent, tells us that Saint Patrick's Bell, the primitive iron clapper bell to be seen in the National Museum in Dublin today, is the same bell used by the great evangelist at his Masses. It has been rung on two occasions since his death, once at the High Mass which marked the high point of the World Eucharistic Congress held in Dublin in 1932, and on the second occasion at the High Mass celebrated in Dublin by Pope John Paul II to mark his memorable visit to Ireland. The actual iron handbell, held together by simple rivets, is one of the oldest relics of early Christian metalwork to survive in Ireland, and in 1090, to preserve it, a beautiful and ornate bell shrine was made for it. According to the inscription on the shrine, it was made by 'Cuduilig and his sons'.

Saint Patrick himself was utterly astounded at the way in which the entire pagan nation of Ireland embraced Christianity. Before his death he saw the whole nation alight with the Faith, a nation of monastic universities and convents which was to burst its Christian banks of fire and flow right through Europe, restoring to it the light of the Faith it had once known before the black-out of the 'Dark Ages' imposed by the Goths and the Vandals. Monastic discipline was the strength of the learning and faith of the monks who went out in their hundreds and thousands to restore Europe to the Faith. They gave Ireland the reputation of 'The Island of Saints and Scholars.'

These spiritual heirs of Saint Patrick were seized with an inner wanderlust such as possessed Saint Paul and Saint Francis Xavier. The strength of Irish missionaries lay in the fact that they carried no imperial flag or national message. They came not to conquer, or to trade, but simply to carry the Cross. They became wanderers in every land, and still remain so today where they live among Africans and Asians, and toil in every nation under the sun. Like Saint Patrick, the Irish missionaries were great orators. Through his message of the Trinity they had fire and joy. They were happy, laughing people, and they brought with them an enormous sense of fun and humour.

Accustomed as we are today to way-out styles, we would, nevertheless, have been amazed at the rig-out of the Patrician missionaries. They wore a white over-tunic of coarse wool. Their tonsure was unique. They shaved their heads across from ear to ear, as the druids used to, in the shape of a half corona towards the front of the head. They wore their hair long at the back of the neck like many a pop star of today. They wore sandals, carried a staff, a gourd for water, and a simple wallet for food and for writing materials. They set up stalls in the market places in the Empire of Charlemagne and shouted joyfully 'Knowledge for Sale!'

Setting up monasteries, they swept through Scotland, Wales and England, and from France to Switzerland, Austria to Italy, and as far as Russia. They were a considerable nuisance to conservative and petty kings, princelings and local bishops, because they caused a certain amount of uproar wherever they went, for many of them were Abbot-Bishops and, like the apostles, they frequently travelled in twelves. They also celebrated Easter in the old-fashioned Paschal Cycle style of Saint Patrick.

One of the results today is that almost wherever you travel you will find a cathedral dedicated to Saint Patrick, be it New York, Melbourne, Auckland or Karachi. These missionaries were more Roman than the Romans, and got little thanks for it until Pope John Paul II recognised their contribution to the world by his pastoral visit to Ireland in 1979.

If ever a writer came near to summing up the life and character of Saint Patrick in a simple, descriptive phrase it was the famous American author, Paul Gallico, who wrote a life of the saint while residing in Ireland at Ashford Castle. He called it, quite simply, *The Steadfast Man*. This is exactly what he was, and in his footsteps trod some of the world's greatest saints, men like Saint Colmcille of Iona, Saint Brendan the Navigator, the first man to voyage to America, Saint Malachi, friend of the great Saint Bernard of Clairvaux, Saint Columban of Bangor and Luxeuil and Bobbio, whose rule almost overtook the Benedictines in Europe for a classical, spiritual way of life, but which was to prove too severe to survive, the philospher John Scotus Eriugena, and the literally thousands of Irish monks, 'wanderers for Christ', who were 'rich in knowledge and poor in money', and who made a major contribution to mediaeval Christian thought.

All this deep spiritual activity was based on the example and teaching of the 'Steadfast Man', Saint Patrick, who tells his own story so vividly in his own words in his *Confession*.

It opens thus: 'I am Patrick, a sinner, the most unlearned of men, the least of all the faithful. My father was Calphurnius, a deacon, son of Potitus, a priest, who lived in the village of Bannavem Taburniae, and possessed a country seat nearby, and it was there I was taken captive.'

It was about the year A.D. 389 that Patrick was born, and in A.D. 404 the Irish pirate raiders swept up the mouth of the River Severn, past the old Roman naval base, and burnt and pillaged the Roman village of Venta Silurum, near the modern Caerwent, where we can still see the outline of burnt ruins today, where once stood its villas, Forum, Curia and Basilica.

Says Patrick: 'I was then about sixteen years of age. I did not know the true God. I was taken into captivity to Ireland with many thousands of people, and deservedly so, because we turned away from God, and did not keep his commandments, and did not obey our priests, who used to remind us of our salvation. The Lord thus made us conscious of His anger and His reprobation. He dispersed us among the nations, as far as the extremities of the earth, to those places where my small efforts still have some effect among strangers. But there the Lord opened up the senses of my unbelief, so as eventually to make me remember my sins, so that I might be converted with my whole heart to God. He gave a glance of pity at my wretchedness, at my youth and my ignorance. He preserved me before I was even aware of it. At that time I was not able to distinguish between good and evil, he came to my help and consoled me as a father does a child...'

Patrick suffered the most colossal and horrific loneliness, tending swine on Slemish mountain in abject captivity, and taught himself to pray night and day. He says, 'When I had come to Ireland, I tended herds every day and I used to pray many times during the day. More and more my love of God and reverence for Him began to increase. My faith grew stronger and my zeal so intense that in the course of a single day I would say as many as a hundred prayers and about as many in the night. I did this even when I was in the woods and on the mountains. Even in times of snow or frost or rain I would rise before dawn to pray. I never felt fatigue, nor was I in any way lazy, because, as I now realise, I was full of the Spirit within me which was fervent.'

Patrick says of himself, 'Whence I, once rustic, exiled, unlearned... was like a stone lying in the deep mire; and He that is mighty came and in His mercy lifted me up, and raised me aloft, and placed me on top of the wall.' After six years of prayer Patrick was undoubtedly a mystic with a deep faith in the Trinity. Then came his escape: 'One night in my sleep, I heard a voice and it said to me, "You fast well, and you will soon go to your own country". Then at the end of some time I once again heard a voice which said to me, "Here is your ship all ready." But the sea was a long way off, it was almost two hundred miles to the port. I had never been there and knew nobody there. But I resolved to run away and I left the man with whom I had been for six years.'

Eventually the fugitive slave was taken aboard by a pagan crew, probably Irish pirates, and tradition has it that the cargo was one of Irish hunting dogs, the huge and ferocious Irish wolf-hounds. After three days of adventure at sea Patrick and the crew reached the coast of Gaul, and for several months Patrick was in his second captivity. Gaul had been rendered barren by the scorched earth policy of the conquering Vandals and Goths, Suevi and Burgundians. This second captivity of Patrick in a desolated Gaul was to last two months. From Gaul he eventually returned to his parents in Britain. He writes: 'And again, after a few years I was in Britain with my parents, who received me as their son, and sincerely besought me that now at last, having suffered so many hardships, I should not leave them and go elsewhere.'

This was not to be, as he writes: 'And there I saw in the night the vision of a man, whose name was Victoricus, coming as it were from Ireland, with countless letters. And he gave me one of them, and I read the opening words of the letter, which were, "The voice of the Irish"; and as I read the beginning of the letter I thought that at the same moment I heard their voice – they were those beside the Wood of Voclut, which is near the Western Sea – and thus did they cry out as with one mouth: "We ask thee boy, come and walk among us once more".

'And I was quite broken in heart, and could read no further, and so I woke up. Thanks be to God, after many years the Lord gave to them according to their cry.'

From A.D. 415 until A.D. 432, Patrick studied Latin and the sacred scriptures in Gaul, probably in one of the great monastic settlements near Tours, and at Lérins, being ordained a priest at Arles. It is highly likely that at the height of the Pelagian heresy he accompanied Saints Lupus and Germanicus to Britain, sent by the Council of Arles, around A.D. 428. It was during these formative spiritual years in Tours and Lérins that Patrick would have become immersed in the spirit of monasticism there, a spirit which he took with him to Ireland and firmly established there. His novice years as a deacon would have been steeped in the old Latin version of the scriptures which preceded the Vulgate of Saint Jerome. Patrick was consecrated a bishop by Saint Germanus, as successor to Palladius. Patrick was created a missionary

bishop without a see until he became Bishop of the See of Armagh.

Of his mission to the Irish, Patrick writes: 'I came to the Irish heathens to preach the Good News and to put up with insults from unbelievers. I heard my mission abused, I put up with many persecutions even to the extent of chains; I gave up my free-born status for the good of others. Should I be worthy I am ready to give even my life, promptly and gladly for His name; and it is there that I wish to spend it until I die, if the Lord should graciously allow me.

'I am very much in debt to God, who gave me so much grace that many people were born again in God and afterwards confirmed, and that clergy were ordained for them everywhere. All this was for a people newly come to belief whom the Lord took from the very ends of the earth as he promised long ago, through his prophets.'

Of the tremendous faith of the Irish converts he writes:

'Hence how did it come to pass in Ireland that those who never had a knowledge of God, but until now always worshipped idols and things impure, have now been made a people of the Lord, and are called sons of God, that the sons and daughters of the kings of the Irish are seen to be monks and virgins of Christ?

'Among others, a blessed Irishwoman of noble birth, beautiful, full-grown, whom I baptised, came to us after some days for a particular reason: she told us that she had received a message from a messenger of God, and he admonished her to be a virgin of Christ and draw near to God. Thanks be to God, on the sixth day after this she most laudably and eagerly chose what all virgins of Christ do. Not that their fathers agree with them; no – they often even suffer persecution of undeserved reproaches from their parents; and yet their number is ever increasing. How many have been reborn there so as to be of our kind, I do not know – not to mention widows and those who practice continence.

'But greatest is the suffering of those women who live in slavery. All the time they have to endure terror and threats. But the Lord gave His grace to many of His maidens; for, though they are forbidden to do so, they follow Him bravely.'

In the concluding words of his *Confession* Saint Patrick writes:

'Behold again and again would I set forth the words of my confession. I testify in truth and in joy of heart before God and His holy angels that I never had any reason except the gospel and its promises why I should ever return to the people from whom once before I barely escaped.

'I pray those who believe and fear God, whosoever deigns to look at or receive this writing which Patrick, a sinner, unlearned, has composed in Ireland, that no one should ever say that it was my ignorance if I did or showed forth anything however small according to God's good pleasure; but let this be your conclusion and let it be so thought, that – as is the perfect truth – it was the gift of God. This is my confession before I die.'

Like Saint Thomas More, another great saint and defender of the right of the individual conscience, Saint Patrick was unjustly accused of taking bribes and illicit payments in the course of his work. In his *Confession* he effectively silences his critics, who must have been a pretty mendacious lot.

Saint Patrick was no mealy-mouthed holy man when his dander was up, and he most certainly tore a strip off Coroticus and his soldiers for their butchery of his newly-baptised converts and those 'newly baptised, anointed with Christ, in white garments', who were sold as slaves and condemned to the whore-houses of the Continent. He condemns Coroticus, a fellow countryman who gave his name to modern Cardiganshire, and calls for his excommunication and boycott. In so doing he reveals much about himself, as the following quotations from his historic *Epistle against Coroticus* show, probably written while he was engaged in his mission work in Leinster and Munster, in the closing days of his missionary life. It begins: 'I Patrick, a sinner, unlearned, resident in Ireland, declare myself to be a bishop. Most assuredly I believe that what I am I have received from God. And so I live among barbarians, a stranger and exile for the love of God. He is witness that this is so. Not that I wished my mouth to utter anything so hard and harsh; but I am forced by the zeal of God; and the truth of Christ has wrung it from me, out of love for my neighbours and sons for whom I gave up my country and parents and my life to the point of death. If I be worthy, I live for my God to teach the heathen, even though some may despise me.

'With my own hand I have written and composed these words, to be given, delivered, and sent to the soldiers of Coroticus; I do not say, to my fellow citizens, or to fellow citizens of the Holy Romans, but to fellow citizens of the demons, because of their evil works. Like our enemies, they live in death, allies of the Scots and the apostate Picts. Dripping with blood, they welter in the blood of innocent Christians, whom I have begotten into the number for God and confirmed in Christ.'

He goes on to say:

'Did I come to Ireland without God, or according to the flesh? Who compelled me? I am bound by the Spirit not to see any of my kinsfolk. Is it of my own doing that I have holy mercy on the people who once took me captive and made away with the servants and maids of my father's house? I was freeborn according to the flesh. I am the son of a decurion. But I sold my noble rank – I am neither ashamed nor sorry – for the good of others. Thus I am a servant in Christ to a foreign nation for the unspeakable glory of life everlasting which is in Christ Jesus our Lord.'

He raises his voice in sadness and in grief for 'Christians made slaves, and that too, in the service of the abominable, wicked and apostate Picts!'

He concludes by saying:

'Where, then, will Coroticus with his criminals, rebels against Christ, where will they see themselves, they who distribute baptised women as prizes – for a miserable temporal kingdom, which will pass away in a moment? As a cloud or smoke that is dispersed by the wind, so shall the deceitful wicked perish at the presence of the Lord; but the just shall feast with great constancy with Christ, they shall judge nations, and rule over wicked kings for ever and ever. Amen.

'I testify before God and His angels that it will be so as He indicated to my ignorance. It is not my words that I have set forth in Latin, but those of God and the apostles and prophets, who have never lied. He that believeth shall be saved; but he that believeth not shall be condemned, God hath spoken.

'I ask earnestly that whoever is a willing servant of God to be a carrier of this letter, so that on no account it be suppressed or hidden by anyone, but rather be read before all the people, and in the presence of Coroticus himself. May God inspire them sometime to recover their senses for God, repenting, however late, their heinous deeds – murderers of the brethren of the Lord! – and to set free the baptised women whom they took captive, in order that they may deserve to live to God, and be made whole, here and in eternity! Be peace to the Father, and to the Son, and to the Holy Spirit. Amen.'

On the Landscape of Ireland three high points blaze out the message of Saint Patrick. They are the Mountain of Slemish, the Hill of Tara, and the Mountain of Croagh Patrick.

Tradition tells us that when he was fasting for forty days and forty nights on Croagh Patrick he wrested from the Good Lord the privilege of being at His side on the Day of Judgement to help judge the Irish Nation. Inevitably, being Irish, they will be late for the last trumpet, but it's a comfort that a dedicated and tenacious and fair-minded Briton will be there to avert from them the wrath of God.

Looking west from the clifftop above Great Stookan, Co Antrim, with the low Mishowen Peninsula in the distance.

Wave and water erosion, and periodic land slips, have shaped the cliffs (above) east of the Giant's Causeway in Co Antrim. Facing page: Benbane Head, east of the Giant's Causeway. Overleaf: (left) a tiny harbour north of Ballintoy, Co Antrim, and (right) the coastal path following the rugged indentations of the north Antrim coast cliffs.

The Giant's Causeway (previous pages), Co Antrim, was formed by the slow cooling of lava from the Cainzoic period, to form basaltic rock split into polygonal columns. Above: Portrush in Co Antrim, built on the narrow arm of Ramore Head. Facing page: sunshine on the field's of the north Antrim coast. Overleaf: (left) a peat-stained waterfall in Glenariff, and (right) farmland near Great Stookan, Co Antrim.

Evening sunlight on Co Down farmland (above), seen from Scrabo Hill, deepens into sunset (overleaf, left). Facing page: pastureland below the Mourne Mountains, Co Down. Overleaf: (right) Scrabo Tower, built in 1851 in memory of the third Marquis of Londonderry, stands on a granite outcrop and is a distinctive landmark of the Co Down countryside.

Roughened water on Spelga Reservoir (above), in the heart of the Mourne Mountains, and off Mahee Island on Strangford Lough (facing page), Co Down. Beyond Strangford Lough lies the narrow, fertile arm of the Ards Peninsula, which ends its twenty-mile length here.

Above: the cathedral city of Armagh, Co Armagh, dates from 443, when St Patrick set up his primatial
See on the hill called Ard Macha. The white, twin-spired Roman Catholic Cathedral of St Patrick
occupies another of the city's hills. Gosford Castle (facing page), built as a large, Norman-style
mansion in the early nineteenth century by Thomas Hopper, stands at Markethill in Co Armagh.

Facing page: storm clouds purple the waters of Lough Erne, and (above) low cloud and rain hide the Coombe Mountains and obscure the outline of Lower Lough Erne, Co Fermanagh. Overleaf: (left) Lough Navar Forest and distant Lower Lough Erne, and (right) Enniskillen, built on an island in the River Erne.

55

These pages: the three rivers of Strule, Camowen and Drumragh meet in the town of Omagh, Co Tyrone.
Overleaf: smaller, faster waterways wind between mossy banks in Gortin Glen Forest Park, Co Tyrone.

The border town of Strabane (these pages), in Co Tyrone, lies at the point where the rivers Mourne and Finn join to form the River Foyle. Overleaf: (left) the Drum Manor Forest Park, four miles west of Cookstown in Co Tyrone. (Right) the dark and snow-dusted mountains of the Sperrin range rise to the north of Cranagh in the Glenelly Valley, Co Tyrone.

Facing page: sunset over the Inishowen Peninsula and the beach at Castlerock (bottom), in Co Derry. Bottom right: the Glenelly Valley, beyond which rise the Sperrin Mountains (below). Right: Mussenden Temple, built by the Earl of Bristol, then also Bishop of Derry, in 1783 on the clifftop at Downhill, Co Derry.

The history of Londonderry (above), on the widening River Foyle, has developed from two decisive royal grants – that of the "Island of Derry" to St Columba in the sixth century, by Aimire, Prince of Hy-Neill, and the granting of the city and county of Derry to the Irish Society of London by James I. Facing page: the resort of Portstewart, Co Derry.

Left: a road through the rough, sheep-grazing land of the Gap of Mamore (bottom left), and (bottom) abandoned farm buildings in the Urris Hills, both on the Inishowen Peninsula, Co Donegal. Below: Lough Swilly, and (facing page) the Atlantic from the rocky coast near Greencastle, Co Donegal. Overleaf: (left) the Grianan of Aileach, an ancient stone fort above Lough Swilly, and (right) farmland below Grianan Aileach.

etterkenny (previous pages), chief town and ecclesiastical capital of Co Donegal, lies on
he mouth of the River Swithy. Facing page: the rocky coast of Doagh Isle, and (above) the
iew across Lough Swilly from the Grianan of Aileach, Co Donegal. Overleaf: (left) Beltany
one circle, and (right) the sandy coast from Bundoran to Kildoney Point, Co Donegal.

Above: evening light on the bay between Dunmore Head and Dawros Head, Co Donegal, and (facing page) the busy fishing port of Killybegs, on Donegal Bay. Overleaf: (left) dry stone walls divide the farmland of Rosguill Peninsula, Co Donegal. (Right) Torneady Point, at the northern tip of Aran Island.

Top left: the Rosses, (left) Rosguill Peninsula, and (top and above) Mulroy Bay, Co Donegal. Facing page: the village of Bruckless, at the head of McSwine's Bay, Donegal Bay. Overleaf: (left) the mouth of the River Glen at Tawny Bay, and (right) Glen Bay and Glen Head, Co Donegal.

St Patrick's Purgatory (above), on Station Island in the inland lake of Lough Derg, Co Donegal,
rivals Croagh Patrick as a place of pilgrimage. The 'purgatory' itself is a cave, now sealed. Facing page
and overleaf, left: the lighthouse on Fanad Head, Co Donegal. Overleaf: (right) Slieve League, Co
Donegal, rises 600 metres from the Atlantic to form the highest marine cliff in Europe.

Rourke Castle (facing page) at Dromahair, Co Leitrim, was once the royal seat Breffni. Top: Lough Ramor, Co Cavan, and (above) Inner Lake, in the Dartrey rest, Co Monaghan. Top right: Cooley Peninsula, and (right) Dundalk Bay, Co uth. Overleaf: (left) Drogheda, and (right) the ruins of Monasterboice onastery, Co Louth.

Right and below left: waterfall at Glencar Lakes, (below centre) Lough Key Forest
Park, Co Leitrim, and (bottom left) fishing boats in Kilkeel Harbour, Co Down.
Bottom right: quiet golfcourse in the countryside of Co Monaghan, and (facing page)
donkeys in the green landscape of the Cooley Peninsula, Co Louth. Overleaf: (left)
Kells, Co Meath, and (right) the Georgian mansion of Headfort demesne at Kells, the
ancestral home of the Marquesses of Headfort.

Co Meath: (top) Headfort demesne at Kells; (above) Newgrange, the main barrow of Brugh na Boinne; (top right) the 12th to 13th-century castle at Trim; (right) market day in Navan, and (facing page) the River Boyne at Slane. Overleaf: (left) the Hill of Slane, and (right) Slane Castle.

101

Below: Lanesborough peat-burning power station, Co Longford. Right and bottom: the green-roofed Church of Saints Peter and Paul, in Athlone, Co Westmeath. Bottom right: Roscommon, Co Roscommon. Facing page: port of Sligo, Co Sligo.

Top: 1,722-foot-high Ben Bulben, in the Dartry Mountains of Co Sligo. Above: Drumcliff Church in Co Sligo, the burial place of W. B. Yeats. Top right: the coast near Moneygold, and (right and facing page) Glencar Lough, Co Sligo.

Below: Downpatrick Head, and (right) Asleagh Falls, near Leenane in Co Mayo. Remaining pictures: the almost timeless farming methods of Co Mayo. Overleaf: (left) Ashford Castle, and (right) Croagh Patrick, a place of pilgrimage overlooking Clew Bay, Co Mayo.

Co Mayo's Killarey Harbour (left and facing page) is considered one of the most beautiful inlets of the Irish coast. Below: the Twelve Bens in the distance beyond Clifden Bay, and (bottom and bottom left) Kingstown Bay, near Connemara. Overleaf: (left) Achill Head and Croaghan on Achill Island (right).

Top: the 15th-century Franciscan Abbey of Moyne, and (top right and overleaf left) Rosserk Friary on the green bank of the River Moy, Co Mayo. Above: Belmullet, and (right) Westport House, near Westport, Co Mayo. Facing page: Ballina on the River Moy, and (overleaf, right) Benwee Head, Co Mayo.

facing page: low, rocky Slyne Head, off the coast of Co Galway, and (above) the sheer cliffs of Inishmore, one of the Aran Islands, Co Galway. Overleaf: (left) the pre-Christian, circular fort of Dun Eoghanachta, lies south of the village of Onaght, surrounded by a web of dry-stone walls dividing the smallholdings of Inishmore (right).

Previous page: (left) summer sky reflected in the still water of Killarey Harbour near Leenane, and (right) a stormy evening sky over Slyne Head, Co Galway. The countryside around Leenane (left), Ballinahinch (below), Roundstone (bottom left) and Ballinakill Bay (facing page) – through which the Dawros River makes its way – is typical of the green beauty of Co Galway. Overleaf: (left) rushing, peat-coloured falls on the Owenriff River, and (right) dark water in Killarey Harbour.

Kylemore Abbey (above), on the shores of Pollacappal Lough, below Doughruagh, Co Galway, was built in Elizabethan style in the late 19th century. Facing page: Ashford Castle, formerly the property of the Guinness family, with Lough Mask beyond, Co Galway. The city of Galway (overleaf), situated on the River Corrib, is the capital of the west of Ireland.

Co Offaly: (top left) Mount Joseph Abbey; (left) Birr; (top and overleaf right) Charleville demesne, Tullamore; and (above) peat cuttings near the ruins of the 6th-century monastery of Clonmacnoise (facing page and overleaf left).

The building of Georgian Castletown House (right), Co Kildare, was begun in 1722 by William Conolly, a speaker of the Irish Parliament. Below: Conolly's Folly, built in 1740 by the Speaker's widow, stands 140 feet high in the grounds of Carton House (facing page), at Maynooth in Co Kildare. Designed by Richard Cassels, the house dates from 1739. Bottom right: St Patrick's College, Maynooth, was founded in 1795 on the site of an older, 16th-century college, and today trains clergy of the Catholic Church. Overleaf: (left) Poulaphouca reservoir, fed by the waters of the River Liffey in Co Wicklow, and (right) rich farmland in hills near Athy, Co Kildare.

Above: the city of Dublin viewed from the southwest. On the bank of the River Liffey stands the old, green-domed Custom House, which now houses the Department of Local Government and the Customs and Excise offices. On the opposite bank lie the quadrangles of Trinity College (facing page and overleaf right). Overleaf: (left) O'Connell Bridge crosses the Liffey into broad O'Connell Street.

The Four Courts (above) has housed Dublin's Courts of Law since 1796, when they were moved there from the precincts of Christ Church Cathedral. The six Corinthian columns of the portico are surmounted by a statue of Moses, with Justice and Mercy on either side. Facing page and overleaf: the Metal or Halfpenny Bridge reflected in the River Liffey.

Top left and top: Phoenix Park Racecourse, and (left) the network of roads south of the Crumlin Road. Above: University College Campus, Dublin. Facing page: Fitzwilliam Square, (overleaf left) Merrion Square, and (overleaf right) St Stephen's Green, Dublin.

cing page: the rectangular layout of Dublin's Trinity College beside the semi-circular
:ade of the Bank of Ireland, formerly the Parliament House. Above: the city viewed from
e east. Overleaf: (left) the River Liffey, and (right) O'Connell Bridge, at sunset.

Left and overleaf left: Leinster House, built in 1745, and the cenotaph to Arthur Griffith and Michael Collins. Bottom left: Dublin Castle, (below) the Four Courts, and (bottom) the General Post Office in O'Connell Street. Facing page: University College, Dublin. Overleaf: (right) St Stephen's Green.

Dublin's fine architecture, evident in the Mansion House (right); the General Post Office (below); the 19th-century National Gallery (bottom); Trinity College (bottom right), and University College (facing page). Overleaf: (left) the Bank of Ireland and Westmoreland Street, leading over the Liffey into O'Connell Street. (Right) the Custom House.

Above: part of the large collection of Irish antiquities in the Kildare Street building of the National Museum, and (facing page) the reading room in the National Library. Christ Church Cathedral (overleaf) was founded by Donat, first Bishop of Dublin, and the Norse King Sitric of Dublin in about 1038. The present building dates largely from the 12th century, and was extensively restored between 1871 and 1878.

Previous pages: Halfpenny Bridge and the River Liffey at dusk. Above: Dublin's Georgian heritage, seen in many grand city doorways. Facing page: the dome and columned portico of the Four Courts, the square spire of Christ Church Cathedral, and the quadrangle and crenellated Record Tower of Dublin Castle. Overleaf: (left) Merrion Square, and (right) O'Connell Bridge.

Facing page: to the south of the River Liffey the Grand Canal describes a large arc from Grand Canal Docks in the east to St George's Church in the west. The statue of 'Eire' (right), by Jerome Connor, stands in Dublin's Merrion Square Park (below). Far right: deer, and (bottom right) fishing, in Phoenix Park, Dublin. The beginnings of Phoenix Park were established by the Duke of Ormonde from the confiscated demesne of the Knights Hospitallers at Kilmainham, and development and planting of the park, which now covers 2,000 acres, began in 1740. Overleaf: the President of Ireland's Residence, set in the green landscape of Phoenix Park.

Facing page: the seaside resort of Greystones, and (bottom left) Enniskerry, Co Wicklow. Near Enniskerry, and backed by the Great Sugar Loaf (below), lies the house of the Powerscourt demesne (left and overleaf), badly damaged by fire in 1974. Bottom: Lough Dan, a corrie lake in the Wicklow mountains.

Top: fields between the town of Enniskerry and Glencree, where (top right) Great Sugar Loaf rises in the distance. Above: gorse flowering in Glendalough Forest Park, (right) falls at Glenmacnass near Laragh, and (facing page) a tumbling stream in the Wicklow mountains.

Above: the harbour of Wexford, with the River Slaney beyond, and (facing page) New Ross in Co Wexford, built on the River Barrow. On the bank of the River Slaney in Enniscorthy (overleaf) stands the turreted castle, built early in the 13th century and now restored and modernised.

Previous pages: (left) the J. F. Kennedy Memorial Park, an arboretum landscaped across the slopes of Slieve Caoilte in Co Wexford. The Kennedy family originated nearby, in Dunganstown. Further east, beautiful grounds surround 19th-century, Gothic Johnstown Castle (right), now used as an agricultural college. Below: Dunbrody Abbey, built east of Waterford by Cistercian monks in c1182. Bottom right: high seas off Hook Head lighthouse, which guards the entrance to Waterford Harbour. East of Waterford, fishing boats crowd into the harbour of Kilmore Quay (right and facing page). Overleaf: (left) the uninhabited Saltee Islands, off the southern coast of Wexford, and (right) the mouth of the River Slaney.

Fields of stubble (facing page) in the Blackstairs Mountain region near Ballymurphy, Co Carlow, and (left) on the plain of Co Laois and Co Kildare. Bottom left and below: views of the Laois countryside from the 200-foot-high Rock of Dunamase, site of an ancient fort. The later castle was reduced to its present ruins by the army of Oliver Cromwell in 1650. Overleaf: the agricultural land around Port Laoise, Co Laois, seen from the Rock of Dunamase.

Above: the undulating land northwest of Kilkenny, Co Kilkenny, and (facing page) meanders in the River Suir, northwest of Waterford. Overleaf: never-ending fields and hedges surround the towns of Inistioge on the River Nore (left), and Graiguenamanagh on the River Barrow, Co Kilkenny.

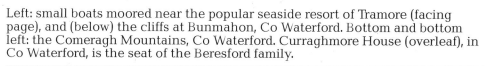

Left: small boats moored near the popular seaside resort of Tramore (facing page), and (below) the cliffs at Bunmahon, Co Waterford. Bottom and bottom left: the Comeragh Mountains, Co Waterford. Curraghmore House (overleaf), in Co Waterford, is the seat of the Beresford family.

207

The dairy farming town of Tipperary (above), on the River Ara, traces its roots back to the 12th century, when King John built a castle here. Older still, however, is the town of Cashel (facing page and overleaf left), whose famed rock was the seat of Munster kings from as early as the 4th century. Overleaf right: Roscrea, Co Tipperary, at whose centre can be seen Roscrea Castle.

Situated in the plain of Tipperary, Cashel is famous for its rock (above and overleaf right) with its Cathedral, Cormack's Chapel, Round Tower and Cross of Cashel. At Cahir, Tipperary, stands the 12th-15th century Castle of the Earl of Thomond and the Butlers (facing page), which was restored in 1840. Overleaf left: the Tipperary landscape and the River Suir, looking southeast from Cahir.

Spectacular though the cliffs of Moore Bay (bottom right) near Kilkee are, they are outshone by the famed Cliffs of Moher (remaining pictures), a five-mile stretch of coastline some 700 feet above the turbulent waters of the Atlantic. Shown perched atop the cliffs (overleaf) is the 19th-century O'Brien's Tower.

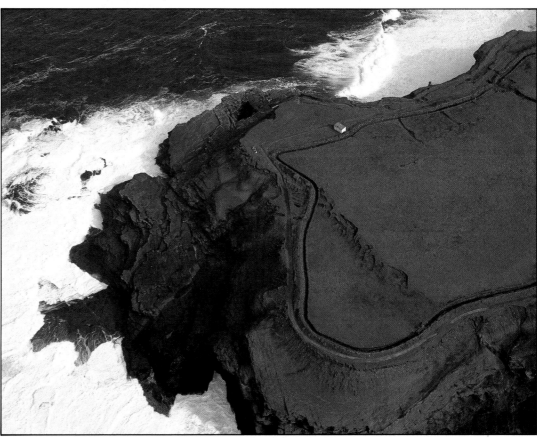

The natural beauty of County Clare (facing page) is well known, but there is also much of interest in the man-made monuments such as Quin Abbey (below), neighbouring Knappogue Castle (bottom left), Bunratty Castle (bottom) and the Craggaunowen Megalithic Centre, a recreation of a Bronze Age complex.

Kilkee (above), an attractive resort town on Moore Bay, lies some eight miles northwest of Kilrush (top), an important Co Clare market town. Also known as a holiday town is Ennistymon, on the River Cullenagh. Top right: the ruins of Quin Abbey and (right) Bunratty Folk Park, in the grounds of Bunratty Castle.

he peace and solitude of a ruined 15th century church (above) near
aherconnell, in the county's Burren region, sums up the tranquility that this
nspoilt county has to offer. Top: a view towards Spanish Point and the distant
tlantic.

Above: the craggy fingers of Sheeps Head, at the southern limit of Bantry Bay and (facing page) the Fastnet Rock and lighthouse, off the southern coast of Co Cork. Overleaf: the plunging cliffs of Mizen Head, southwesternmost point on the Irish mainland.

Below: Ballycotton Lighthouse, on Ballycotton Bay, southeast of Cork. Right: the curved finger of the Old Head of Kinsale, and (bottom right) Knockadoon Head, on Youghal Bay. Bottom: Mizen Head and (facing page) Streek Head on Toormore Bay, southwestern Co Cork.

Among the largest of Ireland's cities, Cork (these pages) stands on the banks of the River Lee and is a major port as well as an industrial centre. The river's two channels are shown (overleaf left) with the city's business heart clasped between them. Overleaf right: aerial view of Cobh and St Colman's Cathedral. The town is located on Great Island in Cork Harbour.

To kiss the famed Blarney Stone is said to bestow upon the individual the gift of eloquence – a quality for which the Irish are renowned. It is this stone, part of the 15th century Blarney Castle (this pages), which largely accounts for the fame of the town. Facing page and overleaf: the varied and beautiful countryside of Co Cork, largest of the counties of Ireland.

Impressionist hues tint the County Cork scenery at Knocknagallaun (top), in the Slieve Miskish Mountains, Adrigole Mountain (above), and Adrigole Harbour on Bantry Bay (facing page). Top right: the ancient, 13-arched bridge at Glanworth, and (right) the bridge over the river Bride at Glenville

243

Timeless scenes of Co Cork: near Skibbereen (top); looking towards the Shehy Mountains from Cousane Gap (above); sheep at pasture in the Shehy Mountain region (top right); rock outcrops near Baltimore (right) and the Dromberg stone circle (facing page), near the famed beauty spot of Glandore.

he Healy Pass road (facing page) snakes through the magnificent scenery of the Caha Mountains
his page), on the borders of Co Kerry and Co Cork. Overleaf: placid lakes and rushing streams
pitomise the unspoilt beauty of the Iveragh Peninsula, Co Kerry.

The magnificent scenery of the famed lakes of Killarney in Co Kerry is shown (facing page and below). Bottom centre: an informative signpost near Moll's Gap, on the Killarney-Kenmare road. Cascades are a feature of the Owenreagh River below Moll's Gap. Overleaf: a fast-flowing river near Castlemaine (left), and (right) the dramatic landscapes to be seen from the Connor Pass.

Left, bottom left, bottom and facing page: the spectacular mountain, lake and shore scenery of the Iveragh Peninsula, and (below) the jagged, foam spattered outcrops off the Dingle Peninsula coast, Co Kerry. Overleaf: the Gap of Dunloe looking north (left) and nearby Upper Lake (right), in Killarney National Park.

Evening light silhouettes the uninhabited Blasket Islands as seen from Slea Head (above), at the western tip of the scenic Dingle Peninsula (facing page). Overleaf: aerial views of the undulating ridges of MacGillicuddy's Reeks (left) and the cloud-shrouded Brandon Mountains (right).

Tiny in proportions, but immensely important as an example of early Christian architecture in Ireland, the Gallarus Oratory (far right) is among the most famous monuments on Dingle Peninsula. Here, other early monuments (right), ancient ruins (above), meandering stone-walls (top right) and remote farmhouses (facing page) blend and become as one with the evergreen landscape. Overleaf left: the beautiful town of Killarney, with the waters of Lough Leane and the peaks of MacGillicuddy's Reeks beyond. Overleaf right: Tralee, principal town of Co Kerry.

When the sun breaks through the clouds, lighting the landscape as at Doon Point, on the Dingle Peninsula, Co Kerry (facing page), it is easy to understand the reason for the name 'Emerald Isle'. This northernmost of Kerry's peninsulas rejoices in some of the most picturesque of Ireland's landscapes, as at Smerwick Harbour, looking towards Three Sisters (left) and Kilmalkedar (bottom left), and (below) Inishtookert Island from Dunquin.

The Ring of Kerry, a coastal road that encircles the Iveragh Peninsula, provides superb views of the countryside, as along its northern sector near Glenbeigh (overleaf left). Overleaf right: the Gap of Dunloe, a four-mile-long pass that runs between the Purple Mountain group and MacGillicuddy's Reeks.

The rugged island of Great Skellig (below, left, facing page and overleaf), with its lighthouse and monastery ruins, is the largest of three that lie some eight miles west of the Iveragh Peninsula. The Bull Lighthouse (bottom) is another of the lights that warn shipping of the county's treacherous coast (bottom left).

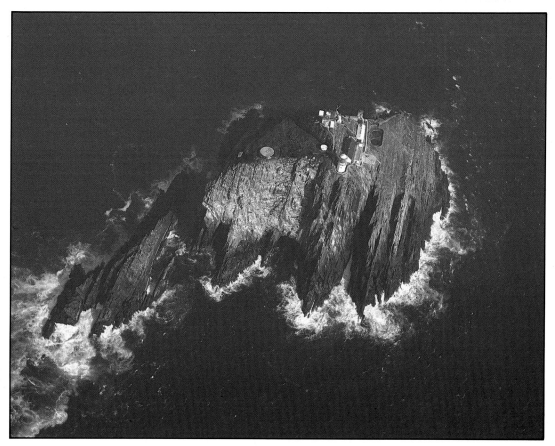

Scenes of Kerry: idyllic (facing page) at Trench Bridge
on Tralee Bay and threateningly magnificent above Connor
Pass (right). Below: a view towards Smerwick Harbour and
the serrated outline of Sybil Point. St Finan's Bay
(bottom) marks the western extremity of the majestic
Iveragh Peninsula whose splendours include the beautiful
lakelands near Killarney (overleaf left) in the east,
and the highlands and patchwork farmlands of
MacGillicuddy's Reeks (overleaf right) at its heart.

1,696-foot Mount Eagle (right) dominates the western tip of the Dingle Peninsula, with its 16th century Dun-an-noir fort (top right) near Smerwick and spectacular Slea Head (facing page). To the east, on the Dingle to Tralee road, lies Connor Pass (top), a precipitous route that offers superb views. Above: MacGillicuddy's Reeks across Lake Caragh on Iveragh Peninsula (overleaf).

Carrantouhill, seen across Lough Acoose (facing page) is the highest point in Ireland, dominating the MacGillicuddy's Reeks landscape (above). To the south, across the Kenmare River (left and top left), on the Beara Peninsula lie the Caha Mountains and the beautiful countryside of the Slieve Miskish range (top).

At 2,713 feet Caherconree Mountain (above) is one of the highest in the Slieve Mish range, on Kerry's beautiful Dingle Peninsula. Further southeast lies Anascaul, which takes its name from 'The River of the Hero' and lies in a hilly setting (left, above and facing page), a few miles inland from Dingle Bay. Overleaf: the rock-strewn landscape of MacGillicuddy's Reeks, on the rugged Iveragh Peninsula of Co Kerry.